Planning Ireland's Future

PLANNING IRELAND'S FUTURE

The Legacy of T.K. Whitaker

Edited by John F. McCarthy

Foreword by Garret FitzGerald

GLENDALE

First published in Ireland by
THE GLENDALE PRESS LTD
1 Summerhill Parade
Sandycove
Co. Dublin

British Library Cataloguing in Publication Data
Planning Ireland's future : the legacy of T.K. Whitaker.
 1. Ireland. Economic development, history
 I. McCarthy, John F.
 330.9415

ISBN 0-907606-81-4

Cover by Gerry Butler
Typeset by Wendy A. Commins, The Curragh
Printed in Great Britain by Southampton Book Company.

Contents

*To my father, John F. McCarthy Jr.,
the finest man I will ever know.*

Acknowledgements

My article in this book first started as an undergraduate thesis submitted in 1969 to the History Department of Princeton University. Many have assisted me during the more than twenty years of this project. My greatest debt is to my former thesis advisor and now friend, Professor Walter F. Murphy of Princeton University. He encouraged me to do further study and made it all possible with grants from the National Science Foundation and the Woodrow Wilson School of Public and International Affairs. I am also grateful to Professor Cyril E. Black of Princeton University for his assistance in arranging this funding. These papers would never have been published without the skill and knowledge of Tony Farmar, to whom I am deeply indebted. My sincere thanks to the following for reading drafts and making suggestions: Henry Bienen, John Blackwell, Basil Chubb, L.M. Cullen, Harold Feiveson, Stefano Fenoaltea, Roy Foster, Brendan Halligan, Shane Hunt, Patrick Lynch, Michael Mahoney, Michael McInerney, James Meehan and John O'Donovan.

I owe special appreciation to those who granted me interviews or who answered my letters, including Thomas J. Barrington, Noel Browne, Tim Pat Coogan, Brendan Corish, Declan Costello, John Healy, John A. Costello, Éamon de Valera, Maurice Doyle, Charles J. Haughey, M. Horgan, Kieran Kennedy, Seán F. Lemass, Frank Loughman, Jack Lynch, Seán MacBride, Seán McEntee, Charles Murray, Dónal Nevin, Séamus Ó Ciosáin, T. Ó Cobthaigh, John O'Donovan, D. Ó Loinsigh, W.J. Louden Ryan, James Ryan, Gerard Sweetman, David Thornley, and T. Kenneth Whitaker. The mere mention of these people does not of course make them responsible for any errors contained in my article.

I am also deeply indebted to my late uncle, Edward Holohan, a former mayor of Bennettsbridge, County Kilkenny, who is responsible for my initial interest in Ireland. I thank my father, John F. McCarthy, Jr (for interviewing Seán F. Lemass and for paying more than his share of my bills), Patrick J. Dineen (for setting up interviews), John K. Kealy (for arranging an appointment with Éamon de Valera and Moore McDowell (for the charts on pages 64-6). Susan C. Jabanoski and Patricia E. Cherrington demonstrated remarkable patience and efficiency in the word processing and administration of this book. Finally, I thank Patricia Dreyfus and Amelia Sandy for editing assistance.

John F. McCarthy, III, Editor
12 April 1990

Foreword

If in any country historians were to describe a political leader as having been responsible for 'a landmark' or 'watershed' in his country's economic history, and a 'revolutionary' initiative, heralding 'a dawn that broke over . . . dismal night', we should indeed wonder who this towering historical figure might be. When these words are applied to a civil servant the reader is impelled not only to a sense of admiration for the figure in question, but also to wonder what kind of society it can have been in which such a role was filled by a member of what normally is a relatively anonymous group of people.

This book tells us much — though by no means all — about the man and it attempts to answer this question about the society in which thirty-odd years ago he came to prominence. Moreover it describes, critically, the aftermath of this seminal event, an aftermath to which it might be polite to apply the term 'anti-climax', some might use blunter language.

Just as it is fair to say that de Gaulle would not have emerged as one of France's greatest leaders but for the special circumstances of June 1940, so also it is no denigration of Ken Whitaker's outstanding qualities of patriotism, imagination, leadership and economic expertise to say that but for the extraordinary circumstances of the late 1950s, he would not have achieved such eminence and public acclaim.

Why did a political vacuum exist at the end of the 1950s that required such an unprecedented initiative at civil service level? I think that we cannot ignore the coincidence of this vacuum with the end of the period of post-revolutionary political leadership. In 1957/58, over three decades after the foundation of the State,

5

de Valera led the Government and seven of his Ministers were also survivors from the War of Independence. (So indeed were the Leader of Fine Gael and several members of his Front Bench.)

Few of the leaders of the nationalist revolution who survived the period of the Treaty and the Civil War had been either radical social thinkers or people with an economic bent; their economic and social views had indeed been conservative even in their youth and, with a couple of exceptions – such as Lemass and McGilligan – their attitudes were even more conservative a third of a century later.

In the period after the Second World War when trade liberalisation was providing a dynamic for growth in the rest of Europe, policy innovation of this kind found few echoes amongst the Irish political elite. Fianna Fáil remained wedded to its inward-looking protectionist stance, which had ceased to yield any dividends in industrial employment or output once the post-war process of developing new industries behind these barriers had been completed around 1950. Industrial stagnation was the result, temporarily masked in the early 1950s by some short-lived opportunistic exports to Britain in the closing stages of that country's period of post-war rationing. Unhappily this was paralleled by equal stagnation in the agricultural sector, the only market for whose products, Britain, was being rendered more unremunerative than ever through the reinforcement of that country's cheap food policy by deficiency payments to its small farming community, now reduced to some 4 per cent of the total workforce.

These adverse conditions for Irish exports were intensified by an excessive deflation of the economy after the Korean War boom, which led to a further bout of excessive deflation in 1956.

As a result of all this, from 1954 onwards, net emigration attained an average level of more than 45,000 a year, equivalent to 75 per cent of the annual birth rate, and when the scale of the consequent population decline was brought to public attention by the publication of the result of the 1956 interim census, the result was a collapse of public confidence in a State which alone amongst the countries of Western Europe was now seen to have achieved economic stagnation at the very time when its neighbours' economies had been expanding at a record rate in historic terms.

It is against this background of universal disillusionment with the political system − far deeper in my view than that experienced during the prolonged deflation which in the 1980s followed the 50 per cent increase in the volume of public spending in the years after 1977 − that the Whitaker initiative has to be seen.

Whitaker's appointment by Gerard Sweetman as Secretary of the Department of Finance followed within days of his paper to the Statistical and Social Enquiry Society on Capital Investment − a paper which provoked a revealing discussion at the meeting in which the recently retired Secretary of the Department of Industry and Commerce, John Leyden, took issue with what he clearly regarded as the heretical views of this Finance official. It was a rare public, (or at any rate semi-public!) display of inter-departmental, and in this instance inter-generational, tensions within the civil service.

At the time of his appointment the country was faced with a balance of payments crisis sparked off by the coincidence of a boom in imports of consumer goods with the final disappearance of the special exports associated with the closing stages of British post-war rationing. To meet this crisis Gerard Sweetman had introduced import levies two months earlier in March. In July, some weeks after Whitaker's appointment, these measures were heavily reinforced by a further set of levies because of what was seen as a failure of consumption to respond to the earlier action.

Then and thereafter this second round of import levies was seen as having been a mistake, precipitated by a failure to wait long enough to see the results of the earlier action. In the absence of published material on this episode, one can only speculate that Gerard Sweetman is unlikely to have undertaken such a politically unpopular move, which contributed to a 20 per cent drop in fixed investment between 1955 and 1957, unless he had received strong advice to the effect that it was necessary. If Whitaker gave such advice, his subsequent actions must be seen in this context − including his later comment that Sweetman was singularly unfortunate in losing office before the ideas which he implemented could bear fruit.

The tensions created by the measures Gerard Sweetman felt it necessary to take during the final year of this Coalition Government are well illustrated by John McCarthy's revelation that only the dissolution of the Dáil on 28 January 1957, in the face of a Clann na Poblachta no confidence motion saved Fine Gael and the Government from a split following a threat of resignation by three Fine Gael Ministers and a Parliamentary Secretary in the face of Sweetman's proposal to cut food subsidies in that year's Budget.

The events that led up to the *First Economic Programme* are described in detail in this book for the first time. These include John A. Costello's speech of 4 October 1956, much of the credit for which must go to Paddy Lynch and Alexis FitzGerald, which proposed export tax incentives and the use of industrial grants not merely as a weapon of regional policy — to attract industry to the West — but also as a means of inducing new industrial development in the country as a whole, and Seán Lemass's similar proposals of 17 January 1957, which were designed to influence conservative forces in his own Party.

It would appear, however, that the first recorded mention within the Government system of 'a comprehensive and integrated programme for economic development' involving 'planning by inducement' as distinct from 'planning by direction' was by Charlie Murray, a principal officer in the Taoiseach's Department who was John A. Costello's economic adviser at the time. His comments were in a response to a memorandum from Seán MacBride, which Murray, however, found unpersuasive in detail. Murray's memorandum, dated 23 January 1957, just two months before the signature of the Rome Treaty establishing the EEC and Euratom, put his own proposals in the context of the possible emergence of a European Free Trade Area within which Ireland's chance of securing special arrangements would, he felt, be better if it had such an economic programme.

At the moment when the second Costello Government was collapsing, and being replaced in March 1957 by de Valera's last administration, Ken Whitaker, in conjunction with Charlie Murray, was launching a detailed study of the Irish economy. In December 1957 Whitaker told his Minister about this study, then well advanced, and secured a Government direction to other Departments to assist with its completion. The first and final editions of *Economic Development* were completed in May and November 1958 respectively, the White Paper based on this document being prepared between these two dates.

It is easy in the light of hindsight to criticise *Economic Development* and the White Paper based on this document. Its reference to 'the virtual satisfaction of (social investment) needs over wide areas' certainly rings oddly in our ears a third of a century later. Its assertion that the dynamic for growth would be found in agriculture, which discounted the problem posed by the absence of remunerative markets arising from the fact that Irish farm products were limited to the unremunerative UK market, was unfounded; the dynamic for growth in the 1960s came from industry. The concern expressed about the disincentive effect of 'high' taxation at a time when it represented only 27 per cent of national income has a nostalgic ring about it at the end of a decade when central and local taxation has absorbed 50-55 per cent of national income. And the growth rate envisaged — a doubling of the 1 per cent growth rate of the years from 1949 to 1956 — proved unduly pessimistic, even allowing for the desirability of setting a low target that could, hopefully, be over-achieved.

But these defects were of limited importance beside the psychological impact of this initiative on a profoundly depressed society and the stimulus to growth provided by the expansion of productive public investment, and by the energies released through the reversal of out-dated and misguided policies. These policies had included restrictions on foreign investment, reliance on protection, and failure to prepare for free trade, and, in the agricultural sector, over-emphasis on tillage as against grassland development.

There was also an element of good timing and good luck; the announcement of the *Programme* happily coincided with a renewed boom in the world — and, specifically, the European — economy, a boom from which Irish industry, encouraged since 1956 to look outwards benefited greatly in the years from 1959 onwards. Moreover the combination of Seán Lemass and Ken

9

Whitaker in the years from 1959 to 1966 was an ideal one from the point of view of fostering economic growth, which in those years had to be not merely the primary, but almost the exclusive, objective of public policy.

In the absence of archival material it is far too soon to pronounce on the years that followed, viz. those from 1966 until the first oil crisis of Autumn 1973. Superficially, once the recession of 1966 had been ridden out, these too were years of economic success; indeed the growth rate for the period may well have been a record for a seven-year period in Ireland. How much of this was a consequence of the dynamic created in the first half of the 1950s, including that within the civil service itself, remains to be seen. It may well have been the case that the momentum of growth in these years obscured a weakening of the political grip on economic policy and a cession of power to a civil service which, not being renewed at the same rate and in the same manner as the political system, tends after a period of high activity to run out of steam.

This, however, is a question to be dealt with by a future generation of Irish historians.

Garret FitzGerald
July 1990

Ireland's Turnaround: Whitaker and the 1958 Plan for Economic Development

John F. McCarthy

. . . I want to see everyone . . . all creeds and classes pro rata *having a comfortable tidysized income . . . That's the vital issue at stake and it's feasible and would be provocative of friendlier intercourse between man and man. At least that's my idea for what it's worth. I call that patriotism.*

Ulysses 526 (New York, 1986)

INTRODUCTION

To anyone passing Leinster House that day, 11 November 1958 must have seemed drearily typical of Dublin's autumn. Rain splashed against the Irish Parliament building's mullioned windows and spattered its limestone façade. Inside, however, the atmosphere was aglow with unusual anticipation as Finance Secretary T. Kenneth Whitaker received congratulations on a project that had taken almost two years to complete. That afternoon, members of the Dáil had received copies of a White Paper entitled *Programme for Economic Expansion*. This White Paper was based on *Economic Development*, a 250 page study of the Irish economy which Whitaker had initiated and supervised. To mark the occasion, the Taoiseach, Éamon de Valera, had invited Whitaker to attend the parliamentary session. As members of the Dáil shook his hand, Whitaker's thoughts drifted back to 1956 when he had begun work on the study that was to revolutionise Ireland's economic thinking. Twenty-eight years later, Whitaker recalled his achievement with characteristic understatement. 'I knew I could put together a team of willing collaborators who would be very able', he said. 'I knew there were

11

people I could touch who would be glad of a release from the rather narrow confines of their own responsibilities. We had econonomists. In the Finance Department itself I brought in as many good officers as I could, no matter what their rank. One must try to transcend the hierarchical system.'[1]

The homeliness of Whitaker's language belies the scope of his vision and the skill with which he wove together the many strands of national aspiration into a cogent policy. He did transcend the system. With a small team of civil servants labouring over statistics and targets, Whitaker visualised the open economy which was soon to bear fruit in fifteen years of unprecedented prosperity for Ireland. He called for the end of protectionism and foresaw the responsibilities and opportunities this growth would create. But, above all, he sat down and worked hard to fill in the detail. *Economic Development* was a key, designed to unlock the wealth of a small nation. And it was successful. What Whitaker did was to outline a blueprint for economic growth, similar to, though not consciously modelled upon, a plan adopted some years earlier by the Commonwealth of Puerto Rico. Incentives – critics would say bribes – designed to attract direct foreign investment in export-oriented, manufacturing industries were the keystone of the plan. Those incentives included government grants to build or expand factories and low rates of taxation on profits derived from the sale of manufactured goods. In later years many countries, both developed and less developed, made similar efforts to create jobs in peripheral areas. In *Economic Development*, Whitaker far-sightedly touched upon themes that the Irish government's Industrial Development Authority would orchestrate throughout the seventies and eighties. Foremost among those themes is the IDA's boast that Ireland is a matchless location for business, especially in the sectors of electronics and pharmaceuticals, because of its geographical location, stability, tax incentives and highly educated labour force.

1956 was a pivotal year in Ireland's history. Whitaker himself gives it the sombre label, 'dark night of the soul'. 'There was a consciousness of our not having made a great go of our own affairs since Independence, and a feeling that we ought to be more efficient. It looked as if all the efforts of nationalists of the past, in achieving political independence, were being turned to nought by our failure to make a go of the place'.[2] Emigration was draining the country's most valuable resource – its people – and at a rate of some 40,000 per year. A heartbreaking process, this often meant final partings for families. The lack of employment opportunities at home seemed in sharp contrast to the better, or at least more profitable, life in other countries. Unemployment came close to 10 per cent by 1957, and the average national income per head was about one-fifth of that in the United States. If the Irish were to be encouraged to remain in Ireland, then living standards would have to approach those available elsewhere. It is a factor increasingly relevant today. In the fifties it placed a crushing burden on what was then an undeveloped economy.

Withered initiative, fear of taking risks, and lack of entrepreneurship had long shackled Ireland's economy. People took comfort in the *status quo*, for all its bleakness, and shunned new methods of farming or industry. According to the eminent American historian, Kerby Miller, throughout the nineteenth and early twentieth century many observers claimed Catholic Ireland still lacked 'industry, thrift, foresight, efficiency . . . while the time-honoured habit of blaming England for all Irish ills remained nearly ubiquitous.'[3] The traditional Irish Catholic view emphasised custom versus innovation, conformity against initiative, fatalism instead of optimism, passivity versus action, dependence over independence and buck-passing in contrast to responsibility.[4] Miller holds that ambitious Irish youths from all classes, aware of traditional Irish attitudes towards individual endeavours and success – the entrenched, peasant-bred hostility to 'upstarts' who aspire to something higher than their ascribed social 'place' – had no choice but to emigrate to a more fluid environment. Another American historian, Joel Mokyr, takes a similar view. Nineteenth century entrepreneurs, scared away by disturbances, insecurity, violence and rural conflict, perceived Ireland as too risky for investments.[5] With emigration heaviest among people fifteen to thirty-five years old, Mokyr asserts that the Irish population was drained of its most resourceful, energetic, ambitious, skilled and educated members. Whitaker was fully aware that Ireland did not have enough native entrepreneurs with the drive, expertise and capital to reverse the country's sagging fortunes. Instead, he looked to foreign companies to provide resources and to the Irish government to create a welcoming environment for the companies, to which Irish young people would otherwise flock for work abroad.

The account of that quiet revolution is inextricably linked with the career and character of Ken Whitaker, whose scholarly appearance and reserved manner gave little hint of the determination within. On 30 May 1956, when he was only thirty-nine years old, Whitaker was appointed Secretary of the Department of Finance. In proposing this appointment to the Government, Gerard Sweetman, Minister for Finance in the second inter-party or coalition government, broke with precedent. He recommended the young Whitaker ahead of senior officials for the most powerful job in the Irish civil service. Sweetman's explanation was simple but convincing: 'Whitaker was the most qualified man for the position. It was that easy.'[6] Despite his youth, T.K. Whitaker had already had seventeen years' experience in the Department of Finance at the time of his appointment as Secretary. He had distinguished himself quite early, working on key documents such as the memorandum which led to the setting up of the Central Bank. Shortly afterwards, in August 1943, he analysed the question of how Great Britain would repay government securities held by Irish individuals and institutions. In April 1949, Whitaker read a paper on Ireland's external assets to the Statistical and Social Inquiry Society of Ireland in which he assessed the nature and value of those assets and discussed the means by which, and the appropriate purposes for which, they might be repatriated. As an assistant principal officer under Finance Minister Frank Aiken, Whitaker had direct and unhindered access to the Finance Minister — a mark of his growing influence within the Department. Whitaker was only twenty-eight when appointed as Aiken's advisor: never before had anyone in the Department travelled so far, so fast. Irish historian, Ronan Fanning, sums up Whitaker's career by quoting a remark made about the British civil servant,

Sir John Anderson: 'Once in a blue moon the open competitive examination for the civil service brings to light a man of his exceptional type who [sic] no power on earth can prevent from sprinting like a flash to the top of the ladder.'[7]

Whitaker's early and middle career was dominated to a degree by one of the longest serving secretaries of the Department of Finance, J.J. McElligott. As a young civil servant, McElligott fought as an insurgent in the Dublin General Post Office in 1916 and was only reinstated in the civil service as Assistant Secretary in Finance in 1923. Though not following the usual form of recruitment to the British Civil Service, McElligott was still a product of the civil service the now Irish Free State inherited from England. The system was based on seniority rather than quality, on time served rather than ambition, and on static rather than dynamic economics. It was, in other words, run by persons who saw their task mainly as accounting. In May 1950 Whitaker prepared a memorandum to McElligott suggesting the establishment of a new Deputy Assistant Secretary post in the Department. The job was to be for him, as he stated directly enough to his boss: 'I suggest – with some modest reluctance – that my experience and capacity could be used with greater all-round benefit . . . if – subject to Mr Redmond [Owen Redmond, then Assistant Secretary] – I were given charge of a general section . . . and the general duty of assisting the head of division and yourself in any problems you might set me.'[8] The new post was to be the seedbed for policy formation, allowing Whitaker and his closest colleagues to develop and explore new economic ideas. It was, in part, an advance recognition of the needs which would reach crisis proportions just when Whitaker took over the reins in 1956.

The Irish government in the fifties was as unstable as the clouds over Galway Bay. Two short-lived political régimes left the Finance Department in disarray. McElligott's long tenure as Finance Secretary came to an end in 1953. His successor, Owen Redmond, left office in 1956, and the second coalition government ousted Fianna Fáil in 1957. Lacking a steady hand at the helm, the Finance Department lost its sense of purpose. As

Whitaker later put it,

> We were drifting along. Nobody was long enough there to accept full responsibility for things. There were quite a number of external crises: the Korean War, the British economy in difficulty and our own balance of payments in deficit. I suppose you can always excuse things, but there was no continuity or responsibility in government for the launching of any comprehensive programme.[9]

Whitaker recognised the need for change, and was eminently prepared to take charge, even though his actual appointment came as a surprise. His reading confirmed the evidence of his eyes: Ireland was rapidly slipping behind other European states. He knew that free trade, with increased competition and the eventual end of protectionism, would become inevitable. He knew also that, to stop emigration, jobs would have to be created by a shift from agriculture to industry and services.

By the time Whitaker became Secretary and took on the key role of running the Department of Finance, he was well acquainted with both its shortcomings and its strengths. His view of his task was a broad one:

> We were trying to respond to very obvious human needs at the time, both economic and social. There seemed to be no prospect of improvement, along the lines we were on, and therefore change was needed. But I would certainly hope myself to preserve as much as possible of continuity with the older values in that transition.[10]

He was dealing in the Department of Finance, as in the civil service as a whole, with institutions badly in need of overhaul and modernisation. He had some success in bringing about change during the course of his swift rise through the Department, but until he took over, the weight of conservative tradition dominated all thinking. Tradition had its merits. The newly formed Irish Free State had inherited a rock-solid system from Britain. Its best standards had been preserved with pride by a body of civil servants, many of whom had moved smoothly from serving the Crown to the service of successive Cumann na nGaedheal and Fianna Fáil governments. Typical of this tradition was Owen Redmond, Whitaker's immediate predecessor, who had joined the service under the British administration in 1906. But the iron-clad administrative practices which made the British system strong enough to work effectively even in the furthest corner of the Empire also made it rigid. Its restrictions were suited to regional or colonial administration which echoed central government, but they were too inflexible for a new country determined to make its own place in the world. Nowhere was this rigidity more evident than in the area of government finance, in which the two basic principles were the minimal budget and non-intervention. Whitaker was to challenge both precepts. Indeed, it could be said that his greatest impact on the country came from setting that challenge and following it up with logical and considered action.

POLITICS OF VACILLATION 1948-1958

Economic Development broke new ground in many critical areas such as abandonment of a protected home market, but it included proposals that were not new, even to Ireland. Between 1948 and 1958 members of the Dáil and key civil servants had urged such devices as low taxes on profits derived from exports, and direct capital grants to encourage foreign investment. Much of Whitaker's plan extended, coordinated or utilised existing state machinery erected during the prior decade. On one occasion an Irish government had even adopted, and published as a White Paper, a four-year national development plan for 1949-53.

Promises Unfulfilled: The European Recovery Programme and Coalition Government, 1948-51
As Europe shook off the dust and rubble of World War II, the *status quo* began to crack under the pressure of change. Ireland was no exception; in the 1948 General Election, a coalition of various Irish political parties ended sixteen years of Fianna Fáil rule. The 1948-51 coalition (the so-called first coalition or first inter-party government) was a strange hybrid of five parties with mutually hostile aims. In a broad if uneasy embrace the coalition contained, on the Right, the pro-Treaty Fine Gael and the Clann

17

na Talmhan representing the farming sector. On the Left were two labour parties and a Republican Party (Clann na Poblachta). Independents of all political hues rounded out the improbable alliance. So heated were the arguments among the partners that, as George Bernard Shaw remarked, the only thing the coalition could agree upon was that they should form a government. In one significant area, however, the coalition did reach a consensus: support for the European Recovery Program (ERP). Fianna Fáil and its leader, Éamon de Valera, the lone surviving commandant of the 1916 Rising, were ambivalent about accepting Marshall Aid dollars, which at that time were the most accessible form of recovery finance. De Valera favoured what he termed 'frugal self-sufficiency' for Ireland, but the coalition saw things differently. Seán MacBride, then Minister for External Affairs, enthusiastically represented Ireland on the Council of the Organization for European Economic Cooperation (OEEC), the coordinating body for the Marshall Plan, in Paris.

As part of the recovery programme the United States Department of State, with the assistance of participating European nations, published a series of 'Country Studies' setting forth the role of each nation. Chapter VIII, on Ireland, declared:

> Ireland's principal problem is the restoration of agricultural production and Ireland's main contribution to European recovery will take place through the production of more food for export. . . . To expand its exports of agricultural products, Ireland needs to mechanize its agriculture, obtain more fertilizers and animal feed-stuffs, increase its imports of fuel and overhaul its transportation system.[11]

The American study expected Ireland to fill the tables of Western Europe with eggs, milk and bacon. The US technicians saw Irish industrial production in a familiar and traditional way. According to this view, industry existed solely as an adjunct to the agricultural sector.

As a further step in organising a joint European-United States recovery plan, participating European nations, including Ireland prepared long-term national economic programmes, covering the years 1948-53. The Irish plan was published as a government

White Paper entitled *The European Recovery Programme: Ireland's Long Term Programme (1949-53)* and as an eighteen-page glossy pamphlet entitled *Working with Europe*, designed for general consumption. Many consider these documents as Ireland's first (and unsuccessful) flirtation with post-war economic planning. In reality they were much less. Instead of offering a comprehensive national economic plan, the primary aim of the proposals was to assure that Ireland, like other European countries, received some US dollars.

The White Paper reiterated the major points of the US Department of State study: Ireland needed dollars to secure imports of grain, feedstuffs, machinery and oil, so that more Irish agricultural products — especially meat, eggs, milk and cheese — could be exported to European nations, especially Great Britain. The 1949-53 plan optimistically called for full employment by 1953, and doubling of agricultural output by 1952. Particular agricultural objectives were noted, including price supports and guaranteed markets and the mechanisation of farming methods.

A more bountiful harvest was just one of the White Paper's targets. Each year, 25,000 acres of trees were to be planted. The State was to finance construction of 60,000 new homes and the erection or extension of 114 hospitals, many for the treatment of tuberculosis. To increase industrial productivity the 1949-53 Programme recommended that the Industrial Credit Corporation provide finance capital for new industries.

For the most part the proposals remained unfulfilled, although the government did use dollar loans and grants partially to finance a policy of state capital investment, mainly in agriculture. In a ten-year (1949-59) land reclamation scheme, started under the Minister for Agriculture, James Dillon, vacant land was made arable through drainage, clearance, fertilisation and the use of new machinery. Marshall Aid loans also paid for farm liming and rural electrification.

This reliance on agriculture instead of industry turned out to be misplaced. It was reminiscent of the policy of the 1920s Irish Agriculture Minister, Patrick Hogan, who once characterised his

economic policy as 'helping the farmer who helped himself
and letting the other fellow go to the devil.'[12] The inefficient
agricultural sector resisted government attempts at modernisation, and agricultural production rose only 8 per cent in the
twelve years 1948-60. As a result, national income increased by
slightly over one per cent per annum in the period 1949-53.
Industrial production remained limited to a few light manufacturing concerns, often owned and operated as family businesses,
geared to the domestic market, and highly protected. The White
Paper did little to help Irish goods compete in the international
market.

Whitaker is candid about the true purpose of Ireland's Marshall
Aid White Paper. It was, he says,

> never conceived of as a programme for policy. It was conceived as
> something to satisfy the Americans so that we would get Marshall
> Aid. It did not have, as far as I know, any commitment of the govern-
> ment to do any of the things. There was simply a group of civil servants,
> of whom I was one, working under the auspices of the Department
> of External Affairs. We were, with MacBride, putting together the
> most plausible memo we could about gradual progress towards a
> more viable economy. We were told that, in order to get aid, you
> have to show that you will be viable in four years' time. So you
> worked to that schedule. But what you were saying had a very limited
> influence on government policy.[13]

Despite its shortcoming *The European Recovery Programme* did
represent Ireland's first attempt to set forth and to publicise
targets of growth for a medium-term period, in this case four
years. Had the private sector and the government backed the
'plausible memo' with serious determination, enabling forecast
to be fulfilled, the original plan might have been followed by a
second, as happened in France with the Monet Plan.

But both the government and the Fianna Fáil régime which
regained power in 1951, ignored the programme in order to
avoid the political embarrassment of being linked to its failure.
The principal value of the ERP was that its abandonment spurred
Whitaker to undertake a far more serious study a few years later.
Nevertheless, the 1948-51 coalition did create two agencies

which were to play a major role in Irish development. One was the Industrial Development Authority (IDA), with an autonomous five-man board, established in 1949-50 to encourage new industries in Ireland. Second, to encourage Irish exports to the United States, the coalition set up the Dollar Exports Advisory Committee in 1950. This led directly to the establishment of a permanent Export Board (Córas Tráchtála) in 1951.

1951-1957 AMERICAN CONSULTANTS AND MINI-PLANS

Marshall Aid for Ireland ended in 1951. The next six years were marked by political upheavals and generally bleak economic conditions. Unemployment, emigration and sluggish growth invited a variety of remedies. Two significant proposals for economic recovery were published during Fianna Fáil's brief tenure (1951-54), neither from the ruling party. One was a report prepared by the New York-based consulting firm, IBEC Technical Services Corporation. The second was a speech delivered at the 1953 Fine Gael Ard Fheis, reprinted in a pamphlet entitled *Blueprint for Prosperity*. During Ireland's second coalition government in 1954-57, political leaders presented four important policy statements dealing with the Republic's economic ills. Three of these were political speeches, later taken up in debate. The fourth and least influential, was a memorandum to members of the government.

Advice From Abroad.
The IBEC Report was an offshoot of the Marshall Plan. In June 1951, the Irish government hired IBEC Technical Services of New York, in conjunction with the IDA, to prepare a survey of Ireland's industrial resources and development potential. The European Cooperation Agency in Washington paid all the dollar-costs (approximately $100,000) while the Irish government met all other expenses. During June and July of 1951, American economist, Stacy May, and his staff interviewed Irish businessmen, trade unionists and bureaucrats. Combining this information with an analysis of available economic dates, IBEC prepared a preliminary report indicating the most promising fields for industrial

development. In a second phase IBEC specialists were to assist the IDA in attracting entrepreneurs to develop those industries. But Fianna Fáil, returned to office in June 1951, showed little enthusiasm for the IBEC study. The Department of Industry and Commerce released the ninety-six page survey, entitled *Industrial Potentials of Ireland: An Appraisal*, in December 1952 but tha promised road led nowhere. The IBEC report was doomed to change nothing but the topic of discussion among academics and civil servants.

Putting the IBEC report on the shelf was consistent with the conservative economic policies of the Fianna Fáil régime of 1951-54. A member of the old guard, Seán MacEntee, again received the portfolio for Finance, a position he had held from 1932 to 1939. At his recommendation, the government imposed new taxes to curb inflation, to discourage consumption of imported goods and to reduce the government deficit. Fianna Fáil agrarian policy was generally a return to the protection and subsidies of the thirties. Wheat and sugar beet received government guaranteed price supports, often leading to surpluses that had to be sold abroad at a loss. The results of these policies were disastrous: the Irish economy stagnated. Few new factories were built or existing ones expanded. Exports and national income made almost no gains in real terms. The cost of living continued to rise and emigration began to reach the enormous proportion of 1881-91.

However, in the later years Whitaker echoed many of the suggestions set forth in the IBEC study. For example, both IBEC and Whitaker's *Economic Development* stressed the need for capital investment in plants and machinery instead of hospital and government housing. Additionally, both documents recognised that Ireland did not seem to have enough native capital know-how or entrepreneurship and so urged promotion of manufactured goods geared for the export market, liberalisation of price controls and encouragement of direct foreign investment through tax incentives such as accelerated depreciation for new fixed asset investment. Similar measures designed to attract multi-national companies were enacted in a 1956 statute an

22

were cited with favour in the Grey Book, as *Economic Development* came to be called after the government published it between grey covers late in 1958 (though Dr Whitaker was always amused by this title since he thought the cover was a light green colour). The 1958 Prices Act, incorporated by reference in Whitaker's study, implemented the IBEC proposal for liberalisation of price controls.

Whitaker disagreed with IBEC's recommendations in some important ways. He took issue, for example, with the consulting firm's proposals to fatten, slaughter and process cattle in Ireland instead of sending them 'on the hoof' to Britain. 'I didn't find much sympathy with such a strangely nationalistic idea,' he stated. 'This [processing cattle in Ireland] is possible only if you get away completely from the British subsidy system.'[14] Whitaker thought that new manufacturing facilities should be located in cities, while IBEC wanted factories established in rural areas. Furthermore, Whitaker saw a need for an expanded Industrial Credit Corporation to provide low interest government loans to industries, while IBEC felt the ICC was largely redundant in a public market supposedly eager to invest in securities. The American study did not specifically mention two tools essential to Whitaker's plan: outright industrial grants and reduced corporate taxes on profits derived from exports. Apart from its substantive economic proposals, however, the IBEC report contained an important practical lesson for Whitaker. It showed him the dangers of making economic surveys and policy recommendations in a policy vacuum. The conservative economies of Fianna Fáil had been at loggerheads with IBEC's innovative ideas. Having seen the stalemate that resulted from such cross purposes, Whitaker was aware that he needed the support, or at least the acquiescence, of elected public officials to implement his proposals in *Economic Development.*

'Blueprint for Prosperity'

In 1953, Fine Gael issued a major policy statement at its annual party conference criticising government policy and offering its own *Blueprint for Prosperity*, the title of a pamphlet that printed the important speeches at this session. Party Leader, Richard Mulcahy, took the traditional *laissez-faire* approach, declaring that, 'The Fine Gael Party stands emphatically for keeping political influence and Government interference out of industrial work'.[15] But former Taoiseach, John A. Costello, whose merry eyes and comfortably jowly face masked an energetic intellect called for a more active role for the state. Costello's proposals included the creation of a vaguely defined Central Savings Office and other incentives to increase savings. He recommended the establishment of a Capital Investment Board to act as a watch dog for public expenditure and its effect on the balance of payments. Another of his proposals was to repatriate capital by persuading Irish commercial banks (which held a large portion of their liquid assets in the form of British pounds and United Kingdom government IOUs) to exchange these assets for liabilities of the Irish Central Bank and Irish government gilts (i.e. bonds). Costello also sought to attract direct foreign investment by removing the restrictions placed on such investment by the Control of Manufacturers Acts. 'The importance of attracting foreign capital particularly of the risk bearing character has not been sufficiently recognised,' Costello warned.

> The sole consequence of the present Statutes is that the best type of foreign enterprise is kept out while any slick merchant who wishes to do so can adopt any one of 100 legal devices of overcoming the Statutes. We should make the economy attractive ground for the employment of capital no matter who subscribes it.[16]

Fine Gael soon had an opportunity to implement its *Blueprint for Prosperity*. The 1954 general election, held in the midst of high taxes and spiralling inflation, resulted in another Fine Gael Farmer-Labour Coalition. This second inter-party government had the support, though not the Cabinet participation, of the three-deputy Clann na Poblachta party. Gerard Sweetman, dapper, abrasive and conservative lawyer with a philosophy of self-reliance and individualism, was appointed Minister for Finance. In 1955–57 Ireland encountered serious balance of payments deficits because of a dramatic rise in imported consumer goods which was not offset by increased revenues from agricu tural exports, tourism or money sent home by Irish emigrants. Sweetman imposed stringent import levies on a number of products in March and July of 1956. The measures were successful in giving Ireland a slight trade surplus the following year. But politically, Sweetman's actions were disastrous. Industrial employment (especially in the building trades) dropped, setting off shock waves of increased emigration, unemployment and massive protest marches. The coalition never had a chance to get off the ground.

The economic nose dive led to the worst economic crisis outside of wartime. People swarmed to leave the country. Emigration rose to an annual average of 80,000, three times higher than the historical average. A sociological study entitled *The Vanishing Irish* summed up the fears of many people that the Irish economy was inherently incapable of sustaining itself. Many emigrated not out of necessity, that is, for lack of a job, but to escape a sense of black despair about Ireland's future. When the census was published for 1961 it would show the population of the Republic at its lowest level ever, down to 2,818,341. Had there been a barometer to measure the public mood there is little doubt that its reading would have matched the census data.

'100,000 Jobs'

With economic conditions so universally bleak, Fianna Fáil, then in opposition, decided to float a trial balloon to test public and party reaction to proposals for revitalising the economy. On 16 October 1955, Seán Lemass spoke to party members at Clery's Restaurant in Dublin, which had become something of a Fianna Fáil clubhouse. His address soon became known as the '100,000 Jobs Speech'. Lemass's speech, as its popular name implies, aimed to create more employment. He outlined an investment programme which would pool some £67 million from the government, along with increased savings from citizens to develop 100,000 new jobs in the private sector within five years. Lemass, an intense but taciturn leader who came to be dubbed 'The Boss', was vague on exactly how the government would pay for this plan. He ruled out increased taxation, and like Costello, sug-

25

gested that 'external assets' – the transfer of bank holdings from British pounds and UK debt instruments to Irish government liabilities – might provide the bulk of the required capital. Lemass also hoped that Irish savings would stop going to finance enterprises in Liverpool and would build factories and offices in Dublin instead.

Months before delivering this address, Lemass, who had served as Fianna Fáil's Minister for Industry and Commerce for nineteen years, had read a newspaper account describing the Vanoni Plan in Italy, a ten-year programme for economic recovery. The article gave Lemass the idea of drawing up something similar for Ireland, and he obtained an English translation of the complete plan from the Italian Embassy in Dublin. Lemass drafted his 1955 speech without a staff of economic advisors to assist him. By his own admission, it was a 'rather amateurish attempt' to emulate the Italian programme.[17] Prior to the talk, Lemass had presented a summary of his proposals to a Fianna Fáil party committee. This committee, unfortunately, did not include heavyweights like Seán MacEntee, a former Minister for Finance, or James Ryan, a former Minister for Agriculture. According to Lemass, some of his colleagues argued that his speech was both unnecessary and unwise: unnecessary because the coalition was already breaking up, and unwise because it would cut off alternative policies. Lemass countered that it 'would be politically wise for Fianna Fáil to try to restore the country's morale regardless of the party in power and that there should be political debate on what measures might bring economic recovery.'[18]

Lemass's cautious speech caused a small furore at the time but it was not the far-reaching economic proposal which Whitaker later produced. For one thing, Lemass's main emphasis was on increased public spending for 'socially useful projects', rather than on funding successful businesses. Fianna Fáil, as Lemass well knew, was not committed to producing a comprehensive economic plan. Nor was Lemass speaking for the entire party when he asserted that 'the primary aim of Fianna Fáil was to increase the nation's wealth and to improve the living standard of the people.'[19] The '100,000 Jobs Speech', as Lemass later contended, 'promoted public acceptance of the idea of programming, planning and active government intervention to eventually produce a pre-defined economic plan.'[20] While the speech outlined no such plan, it did have a considerable impact at the time. In later years it acquired the aura of a legendary breakthrough in Ireland's economic development. Lemass helped the folklore along by conforming to the image of a skilful and determined economic manager, the role for which he is mainly remembered.

Though he recognised his limitations as an economist, Seán Lemass brought a new force to Irish politics with his pragmatism. This contributed to the shift in emphasis away from objectives like the restoration of the Irish language or the reunification of the country, and towards the bread-and-butter business of making the country more prosperous. In his various proclamations Lemass provided ammunition for friend and foe alike. His '100,000 Jobs Speech' violated American columnist, Jane Bryant Quinn's rule about staying alive as a forecaster: produce a number or a date but never both at once. In the debates over Fianna Fáil's 1958-59 Budget, a Fine Gael spokesman asked Mr Lemass why the one-year-old government had not produced the first instalment of 20,000 new jobs. James Dillon, former Fine Gael Agriculture Minister, quipped that Lemass would indeed provide 100,000 more jobs, but the work would be in Boston and Birmingham. On the other hand, certain Fianna Fáil members have exaggerated the importance of the Lemass speech. Replying to a question about the origins of economic planning in Ireland, Seán Lemass's son, Noel, maintained 'Seán Lemass laid down the programme in Clery's Ballroom in 1955.'[21] A Fianna Fáil Minister enthusiastically seconded the notion: 'Fianna Fáil's adoption of the concept of economic development programmes was first announced by Seán Lemass at a meeting in Clery's on 11 October 1955.'[22]

'Policy for Production'
Whatever its ultimate impact, Lemass's '100,000 Jobs Speech' generated a heated debate within the Fine Gael party about Ireland's economic situation. Addressing a special inter-party meet-

ing on 5 October 1956, the Taoiseach, John A. Costello, delivered the government's reply. It was his final, though unsuccessful, attempt to keep the crumbling coalition together and was later published by Fine Gael in a pamphlet entitled *Policy for Production*. Fine Gael, like other Irish political parties in the fifties, vacillated over the government's proper role in economic matters. The preface to the pamphlet pointed out the danger of the 'growing power of the state' and suggested government action 'to achieve the desired result by cooperation rather than by compulsion.'[23]

Considering Fine Gael's traditional orientation towards agriculture, it was not surprising that Costello, echoing Hogan yet again, concentrated on steps to revive that sector by reiterating words from a speech he delivered in July 1955: 'It is to agriculture, primarily, we must look for that essential prerequisite of economic progress. . . .'[24] Costello proposed three measures to buttress farming as the country's economic foundation. First, he urged the establishment of an 'Agricultural Production Council' with representatives from government and farming associations. Its aim would be to increase farm output. Second, he looked for the formation of an 'Agricultural Institute' to promote agricultural education and research. Finally, he sought expanded credit facilities to finance farm improvements which would increase production. A major failing in Costello's policy for agriculture, as economists such as Patrick Lynch were later to argue, was its insufficient market orientation. It was guilty of the economic fallacy that 'what you can produce you can sell.'[25]

Costello's recommendations for industrial growth were far more significant. He proposed two new devices: tax incentives to encourage exports and government grants to encourage investment in plants and factories. These same tools formed the foundation for the 1958-63 Whitaker Plan. Costello proposed halving the corporate income tax on profits from increased exports of manufactured goods over the levels set in a base year. He also announced a government programme to provide grants up to two-thirds of the cost of construction for new factories in rural areas. To be eligible for these grants, industries would have to be 'essential to the national economy' and make goods not already produced in Ireland.

While their fundamental concepts were the same, two important differences distinguished Costello's and Whitaker's approaches to tax incentives. Costello relied on Irish businessmen to expand or establish manufacturing concerns. Capital, he felt, would come from increased Irish savings, from repatriation of foreign stocks and bonds held by Irish citizens and, to a lesser extent, from the Industrial Credit Corporation. Whitaker, revealing either less optimism about his countrymen's enterprise or greater foresight, stressed the need for companies from New York and Hamburg to invest in Ireland. A second distinction between the two approaches is the degree of economic sophistication evident in each policy. Whitaker bolstered his own expertise with that of a team of civil servants and economists. Costello, by contrast, relied only on his son-in-law, lawyer Alexis FitzGerald,[26] and economics professor Patrick Lynch for help in preparing his speech. Prior to delivering the speech, Costello did not even discuss it with any member of the coalition government. 'I had been fully aware that unless we produced a plan soon we were heading for trouble', he recalls.

> In order to cope with the balance of payments difficulty we put levies on imports that caused unemployment. I felt there should be some economic plan to deal with the situation, something constructive to coincide with the strong measures we were taking. We had to give the economic body a tonic as well as medicine.[27]

Trades unions and farmers' associations responded to Costello's speech with admiration and respect. But such was not the case in political circles. Éamon de Valera publicly heaped contempt upon Costello's proposals. 'The Taoiseach has treated us to another of his coalition blueprints for prosperity tomorrow,' mocked de Valera. 'If professions, programmes and promises, with commissions, councils and consultations were a cure for our ills, or a substitute for decision and effective action, this country should never be in bad health.'[28] The Fianna Fáil attack was expected, but dissatisfaction among members of the Dáil, who heretofore had supported the coalition, brought down the second inter-party government within a few months.

Lemass Plan – Part II (January 1957)

Despite Éamon de Valera's criticism of government economic initiatives, his Fianna Fáil party soon issued a detailed policy statement in response to the Costello Plan. On 17 January 1957, Seán Lemass addressed members of Fianna Fáil in Dublin and proposed an increase of 12 per cent in national production. Wisely choosing discretion over valor, Lemass did not specify how the increase would come about nor how long it would take. In contrast to his earlier address, Lemass this time included the agricultural sector, with recommendations similar to Costello's. Like his Fine Gael opponent, Lemass based his proposals on the premise that agricultural exports must increase. 'So long as there is freedom for families to move to Britain, our standards must approximate to British standards, or our population will go,' he warned. 'It is the survival of the nation which is involved, and not merely our living standards, unless we can achieve by our own efforts, a rapid and substantial increase of our resources.'[29]

To achieve this aim, he echoed many of Costello's suggestions: a board to encourage agricultural marketing, a bovine TB eradication programme, an agricultural bank to provide better credit facilities for farmers and increased availability of technical knowledge. Lemass also reiterated many of Costello's proposals for industry. First, and most important, he suggested cutting taxes on profits derived from exports of manufactured goods. He also favoured allowing the portion of profits derived from exports to be tax-exempt for a number of years. 'I am convinced,' he predicted accurately, 'that the prospect of tax-free profits on exports will prove a powerful magnet.'[30] Other Lemass proposals included linking Irish firms with larger companies that could supply capital, technology and connections, and consolidating smaller companies with the help of the Industrial Credit Corporation. He also called for the establishment of a commercial export board for industry, similar to the one for agriculture. To finance these programmes, Lemass proposed a £60 million government investment. The money would come, directly or indirectly, from Irish citizens' pockets. 'Everybody who is not unemployed,' said Lemass, 'must be prepared to reduce his personal consumption expenditure by above five per cent − voluntarily, by saving, or involuntarily by taxation − to make the resources available.'[31] He gave no details as to how much would be spent each year or how much would go to each project.

As in his 1955 speech, Lemass did not seek to voice the policy of the entire Fianna Fáil party. He was trying instead to influence, and possibly convert, the more conservative members of the party, especially Seán MacEntee. A favourable response to his address would give Lemass more ammunition to win over the party to his economic policies. He hinted at this intra-party struggle when he introduced his speech as 'indicating the ideas that are now being discussed within the party rather than a finalised programme.'[32] Lemass's 1957 speech, delivered on the eve of a general election, summed up Ireland's far-reaching economic challenge. 'This country cannot afford to drive its people away by deliberately depressing trade and employment', Lemass declared. 'Apart from the loss of productive personnel, the effect on national morale is critical. The restoration of confidence in the country's future is an essential part of the whole campaign for economic recovery.'[33]

The MacBride Plan

While Lemass and Costello were making public addresses in 1956-57 on how the government should deal with the Irish economy, a third politician was trying to formulate government policy behind the scenes. Throughout 1956, Seán MacBride and his Clann na Poblachta party had become increasingly critical of the second coalition. Their dissatisfaction carried weight, for small though it was, Clann na Poblachta provided the support necessary for the coalition to retain its slim parliamentary majority. An ex-IRA chief-of-staff with handsome, chiselled features, MacBride believed that the government lacked a comprehensive policy to deal with the high rate of unemployment. During the first half of 1956, he privately suggested to the government that the co-alition adopt a long-term programme for economic recovery. The conduit for MacBride's ideas was usually John O'Donovan, the Parliamentary Secretary who acted as a liaison between MacBride and the government.

MacBride had been interested in economic planning ever since he had participated years earlier in a survey of Italy, Turkey and Greece by the Organization for European Economic Coopera-tion (OEEC). A forceful and dominant personality, MacBride did not hesitate to use pressure when persuasion seemed ineffec-tive. On one occasion, according to Ronan Fanning, Whitaker vividly remembered him 'sitting astraddle on a chair in the middle of the room (with other members of the government sitting around the sides) and relentlessly cross-examining his senior Finance colleagues, a process which began at two o'clock in the morning.'[34] Getting no response to his private appeals for an economic development plan, MacBride advised the second co-alition that he would take his case to the public. On 9 July 1956, he tabled a motion in the Dáil calling for the formulation of a coordinated programme. When no time was allotted to debate this motion, MacBride drew up a twenty-six page outline of his own proposals for an economic plan modelled on ones adopted in Italy, Turkey and Greece. In the autumn of 1956 he circulated two or three hundred copies of his memorandum to Cabinet members, inter-party deputies and other interested persons. It was entitled 'Brief Memorandum on Need for a Ten-Year Econ-omic Development Plan and on Method of Formation'.

The MacBride mini-plan did not attempt to present detailed proposals for an economic plan. Instead, it sketched the pro-cedure that should be followed in formulating such a plan. Like Lemass in his '100,000 Jobs Speech', MacBride called for higher employment, with a target of 30,000 additional jobs over a ten-year period. But unlike previous proposals, MacBride stressed the need for a comprehensive government policy to coordinate the work of various departments. The Clann na Poblachta leader recommended the appointment of a two- or three-man team to draw up a rough draft of an economic plan. Economic and financial experts would then study this draft and a revised version would be submitted to the OEEC, which MacBride hoped might help pay the bill for the plan. Other potential sources of funding were private investment, the International Monetary Fund, the World Bank and postponement of Marshall Aid repayments. To administer the plan, MacBride called for the government to create a new planning section separate from any existing department. Finally, he proposed sending approximately twenty young Irish economists to continental Europe to study various plans. Mac-Bride's memorandum was the clearest proposal to date by any elected political actor for adopting some form of a West European national economic programme in Ireland. But his ideas received little support. Sweetman rejected the memo out of hand and characterised it as 'certain suggestions which could not be classified as an economic plan.'[35]

While Sweetman spurned MacBride's suggestions, John A. Costello was more receptive. He told MacBride of his interest and promised to respond later. Costello sent a copy of the memorandum to his friend John Vaizey, a Cambridge University professor of economics, for comments. But academic demands or other concerns apparently came before Irish economic policy. Weeks dragged by without the Taoiseach receiving any reply from the Cambridge don. Before Costello could answer MacBride, the coalition government had fallen.

MacBride is the most controversial figure among the men who endeavoured to launch Irish economic planning. He was well-connected, with contacts throughout Europe. His work with the architects of OEEC planning conferred authority within the government. Not surprisingly, given the instability of a multiparty coalition, he had additional authority as the leader of one of the member-parties. Unlike Lemass and Costello, MacBride gave his proposals an international flavour from the start, owing in part to his former position as Minister of the Department of External Affairs. But his political thinking was too radical, favouring investment in social programmes without much concern for the productivity requirements which governed thought within the Department of Finance.

The General Election of 1957

Ironies abounded in the defection by Clann na Poblachta from the second coalition. On the weekend 25-7 January, the executive board of MacBride's party met to discuss its support for the government. MacBride had only recently returned from New York, where, as the Irish representative on the Council of Europe, he had discussed the Cyprus question in the United Nations. He was surprised to learn how dissatisfied his tiny party had become with the coalition. At the time, the IRA was waging an armed campaign in Northern Ireland blowing up customs posts, police stations and power generators. Many Clann members had been active in the IRA during the thirties and forties. MacBride himself had been the chief-of-staff of the IRA in the late twenties and early thirties. It was therefore inevitable that, when John A. Costello ordered the arrest of suspected members of 'illegal organisations' in early January 1957, his days as Taoiseach were numbered.

Although MacBride was one of the severest critics of the second coalition at his party's weekend conference, he nonetheless urged continued support of the government. He argued that a new Fianna Fáil régime under Éamon de Valera would take even more stringent measures against the IRA. Ignoring MacBride's warning, the Clann voted rank and file to withdraw parliamentary support. On 28 January 1957, MacBride followed his party's instructions and introduced in the Dáil a motion of no-confidence in the government. As reasons, he cited the coalition's failure to deal adequately with partition and its handling of economic policy.[36] Rather than face a vote of no-confidence, Costello asked the President to dissolve the Dáil. A general election was fixed for 5 March 1957.

The 1957 General Election campaign opened on a sour note for all coalition parties. Fine Gael was divided and tired: divided over Sweetman's unpopular deflationary economic measures, such as cutting the budget and scaling down social services, and tired after two-and-a-half years of narrow parliamentary majorities. Labour was racked with cries from left-wing members that the party had not pushed hard enough for progressive social and economic legislation. As for Clann na Poblachta and the farmers' party, Clann na Talmhan, they had become little more than an ill-assorted collection of independent deputies.

Single-party rule to replace a coalition administration was the crucial issue in the 1957 campaign. In response to a questionnaire sent in the autumn of 1968 to all successful candidates in the 1957 General Election, eighteen out of twenty successful Fianna Fáil deputies indicated that 'return to a single party government' was the most important question facing the electorate. Since Fianna Fáil had been the only political party since 1932 capable of achieving an absolute parliamentary majority, advocating a single-party government simply meant supporting them. During the campaign, Fianna Fáil complained about the economic conditions of the country but failed to spell out alternative policies. For most voters, the 1957 election was merely another opportunity to affirm old loyalties formed during the civil war.

Fianna Fáil's economic platform was, at best, ambiguous. Although the party's élite had discussed the issue among themselves during the campaign, the party as a whole avoided taking up a public position. Privately, Seán Lemass and others had urged support for his 'national recovery' plan, but according to Lemass no consensus had been reached: 'The general tenor of our campaign was that the serious economic difficulties of the times were curable and that Fianna Fáil had developed ideas for effecting a comprehensive cure,' he recalled later. 'We did not elaborate on these ideas on which our collective mind was not at the time, fully made up.'[37] As Irish political scientist, Peter Mair, has noted, Charles Haughey in the 1987 election campaign echoed the calls of his father-in-law, Seán Lemass, in 1957, that Fianna Fáil was the only party capable of forming a government on its own.[38]

Although he had presented a major address on economic policy a few days before the dissolution of the Dáil, Lemass virtually ignored that speech in his campaign. Fine Gael forced him instead to defend himself against allegations that he favoured forced, Stalinist-type planning. In a radio broadcast, Lemass replied:

'We in Fianna Fáil do not believe in the methods of compulsion in this situation. Compulsory tillage, the regulation of wages, undue control of private business – none of these form any part of our plan.'[39] Clearly, de Valera and Fianna Fáil's conservative wing, especially Seán MacEntee, did not want a growth-oriented, interventionist economic policy creeping into the party's platform. One member of the Fianna Fáil leadership, former Agriculture Minister, James Ryan, said that the party 'felt Ireland was not ready for a plan at that time.'[40] The Irish economy might have needed such a plan, but the conservative Irish electorate, Fianna Fáil felt, would reject it.

On the other side of the political fence, Fine Gael gave lip service to the Costello Plan of the previous October, but its leaders worried more about confirming the party's commitment to free enterprise. Gerard Sweetman was explicit in his affirmation: 'We reject socialism with its planned direction of the capital and labour as being foreign to the Irish way of life.'[41] John A. Costello took a similar position. Again Peter Mair points to the curious parallels between the 1957 and 1987 election. In both contests, Fine Gael stressed the Ronald Reagan ideals of less government interference in the economy and more reliance on private initiative and the free market.[42]

Meanwhile, Fine Gael's coalition partner, the theoretically socialist Labour Party, did not even mention long-range economic planning in its election manifesto. Some Labour candidates did support the proposals published in a trade union pamphlet, *Planning Full Employment*, published in December 1956. This pamphlet presented 'a trade Union viewpoint on the measures which should be taken to overcome, as rapidly as possible, Ireland's economic difficulties.'[43] These measures included various government incentive packages such as lower taxes on profits derived from increased exports and grants to new industries producing wholly or mainly for export. Most Labour candidates ignored the pamphlet. The Labour Party was to move leftward in the 'socialist' sixties, but in 1957 Ireland was the only country in Western Europe whose three major political parties were conservative on economic matters.

MacBride's Clann na Poblachta, the only group advocating some form of economic planning during the election campaign, was decimated at the polls. Seven days before the balloting, MacBride had argued that 'nothing short of an agreed, comprehensive long-term economic programme could enable the country to survive economically.'[44] MacBride, however, lost his seat for the constituency of Dublin South West, which he was never to regain, and his party's representation in the Dáil fell from three to one.

Instead of voting for specific policies, a large portion of the electorate cast protest votes against the bleak economic situation. Fianna Fáil, as the party out of power, benefited most, winning 48.3 per cent of the valid first preference vote, a virtual landslide by Irish standards. Fianna Fáil had seventy-eight seats, giving them a manority of nine. This effectively became thirteen when four Sinn Féin deputies refused to take their seats in what they jeeringly called a 'partition' parliament. Sympathy for two young IRA men, killed in a January 1957 raid on police barracks in Northern Ireland, was largely responsible for the victory of these four Sinn Féin candidates, some of whom were in jail at the time. In one Dublin constituency, a candidate claiming to represent unemployed workers and who was himself unemployed, won a seat and a job.

Since Fianna Fáil did not put forth any detailed economic policies, the 1957 election was not a referendum for any particular government action regarding the economy. As Seán Lemass admits, 'It is true that we did not seek in the General Election of 1957, a specific mandate for economic planning.'[45] The one or two Fianna Fáil members who did have some ideas on this issue were not allowed to present them to the electorate during the campaign. Perhaps that posture was politically sound, since the 1957 electorate rejected any candidate who voiced support for any form of economic planning. Yet within twelve months the new Fianna Fáil government would publish a sweeping programme of economic changes which later would be lauded as having turned around the Irish economy.

EVOLUTION OF ECONOMIC DEVELOPMENT

As the new Finance Secretary, Ken Whitaker was aware of the numerous calls for an overhaul of Irish economic policy between 1948 and 1957. The clamour for change came from diverse sources: international consultants, political figures as antithetical as Seán MacBride and Seán Lemass, the trades unions, the Labour Party and various academics, such as Patrick Lynch. More importantly, Whitaker was conscious of the growing acceptance of economic planning in post-war Western Europe. For years such planning had been suspect because of its ties to left-wing ideology, a handicap more compelling in Ireland than elsewhere. Whitaker later explained:

> There is no doubt at all that in the early 1950s the concept of planning was bedevilled by this association with socialist, communist regimes. The idea of democratic planning became acceptable only later in the fifties and against the background of the French example where it was seen to have a relevance to Western democratic forms of government as well.[46]

Whitaker argued that a plan should not be 'a rigid framework imposed on the community by an authoritarian government.' Rather, he said, it should grow out of a recognition by modern democracies of the need

> to organise development systematically, to provide an increasing number of better-paid jobs for an increasing number of better-qualified workers; to rationalise the system of production in preparation for the more difficult conditions ahead. A modern community is concerned with collective as well as private spending; with the structure of education and its adequacy in relation to the world of tomorrow, and with the provision made for other social needs such as housing, health, social welfare and communications.[47]

Whitaker was a keen student of French planning. The Monet Plan (1946) was launched jointly with Marshall Aid, like the reconstruction efforts of other countries. He was also aware that key government figures, even in Ireland's conservative political culture, were increasingly receptive to some form of planning.

Lemass, for example, had studied the 1954 Vanoni Plan in Italy and MacBride had helped formulate the Greek and Turkish plans in conjunction with OEEC. Whitaker knew that no policy would have a practical effect unless the government approved, launched and implemented it. The growing respectability of comprehensive national plans in democratic countries made it easier for Whitaker's proposals to be adopted.

Something else was afoot in Europe that also influenced Whitaker: the development of the Common Market. In 1957 British entry into the European Economic Community seemed imminent, a move the Irish regarded with some apprehension. If Ireland joined the European Community together with the United Kingdom, the protected, often inefficient Irish industries would be hard pressed to compete within a free trade area. But self-imposed isolation from the British and European markets was out of the question. Ever since the trade agreements of 1938, Irish agricultural products had enjoyed preferred treatment in England. This advantage would be lost in a European Economic Community with a protectionist common agricultural policy. In his opening chapter of *Economic Development*, and again in an appendix, Whitaker declared that Britain's prospective entry into the EEC underlined the urgency of the Irish economic situation. 'The possibility of freer trade in Europe . . . necessitates also a re-appraisal of future industrial and agricultural prospects,' he wrote. 'It seems clear that, sooner or later, protection will have to go and the challenge of free trade be accepted.'[48]

Despite the constellation of external factors pressing Ireland to take economic action, an even greater stimulus came from the country's pervasive mood of gloom and despair. Whitaker was saddened and depressed by Irish emigration, unemployment, population decline and economic stagnation. The picture looked even bleaker when contrasted with the rapid economic growth of other European countries. It disturbed Whitaker that three and a half decades of political independence had done nothing to reverse the trend of mass emigration and unemployment. As one of his colleagues noted, 'Certainly the persistently high levels of emigration and unemployment would have been a source of great

39

worry to a civil servant occupying the responsible position of the Secretary of the Department of Finance.'[49] Another Finance Department official maintained: 'The factor that weighed most heavily on the mind of Whitaker was the 30,000 Irish who emigrated annually.'[50] Whitaker best expressed his feelings when he himself observed in *Economic Development* that 'after thirty-five years of native government people are asking whether we can achieve an acceptable degree of economic progress.'[51]

A declining population, Whitaker reasoned, had certain budgetary advantages: the government could reduce spending for public housing, hospitals and other social services. But any savings would be offset by the increased unemployment that would result from such cutbacks. In a note to James Ryan, Minister for Finance, in December 1957 Whitaker recorded his concern: 'A slowing down in housing and other forms of social investment must be faced from now on because of the virtual satisfaction of needs over wide areas – and it is necessary to find productive investments which will prevent the unemployment problem from becoming very serious.'[52]

The poor performance of the Irish economy could not escape unflattering comparisons with other nations. The OEEC published yearly reports that alerted Irish economists to the progress being made throughout Western Europe. Dr W.J. Louden Ryan, who helped prepare the *Second Programme of Economic Expansion*, recalled: 'The statistics published by OEEC gave us a greater awareness of how one country compared to another. We began to ask ourselves why we alone were not growing.'[53] Whitaker exemplified this wider consciousness among professional economists. Throughout *Economic Development* Whitaker compares the stagnant economy of Ireland to the remarkable growth in Western Europe, Canada and the United States.

To a new class of Irish economists and business leaders, greater awareness of other countries' economic performances went hand in glove with increased receptivity to outside influences in general. Although Ireland had received only a small amount of Marshall Aid, officials attended the discussions which preceded the formation of the OEEC. Ireland tended to drag her feet in these initial meetings, but exposure to fresh ideas 'stimulated new thinking and the emergence of new attitudes toward development policy.'[54] Whitaker put it dramatically and succinctly by pointing out: 'We now lag so far behind most other European countries in material progress that even a spectacular increase in efficiency and output will leave us at a relative disadvantage.'[55] A decade later, Whitaker summed up the economic malaise of the mid-fifties: 'We had a feeling that we got through a crisis in the balance of payments with great despondency and discouragement. Emigration had been high and the rate of growth low, and everything seemed to have been going wrong. People were very low psychologically at the time.'[56]

Like a small boat in a hurricane, Ireland in 1958 was heading rapidly toward crisis. It was Whitaker who grabbed the tiller and set a new course, drawing about him people who shared his concern about the state of the nation and who were able and willing to act. Out of all of this, *Economic Development* was born.

Recruitment and Formulation

The preparation of *Economic Development* had three distinct phases. First came Ken Whitaker's initial research, followed by his recruitment of staff to work both directly and indirectly on the project. The final step was the drafting, editing and combining of chapters. 'There was that great feeling of a team, of everybody being willing,' Whitaker claimed. 'Nobody asked for any special exemption from current duties to do this. They just joined in and worked overtime on it as we all did, looking forward to the next day to get cracking.'[57]

Years before his appointment as Secretary of Finance, Whitaker had already begun to explore the ideas he was to develop in the Grey Book. During the early months of 1956, Whitaker took it upon himself to assemble some facts and figures on Ireland's Gross National Product (GNP), capital formation and savings. The fruits of his research ripened into a paper, entitled 'Capital Formation, Savings and Economic Progress', which Whitaker presented on 25 May 1956, before the Statistical and Social Inquiry Society,[58] an organisation made up largely of Irish economists from business, government and academe. Dry and hard-slogging, Whitaker's economic pronouncements did not cause great excitement throughout the pubs of Ireland. Yet the paper heralded both the message and the medium of his later contributions. The paper made three principal recommendations which Whitaker later elaborated, refined and developed in the Grey Book. Briefly stated, his conclusions were that firstly, national output needed to be increased and more of it devoted to plants and factories; secondly, savings should be increased and used as productively as possible; and thirdly, savings should be encouraged by lowered taxes and a more liberal attitude towards profit-making.

In addition to the paper's prophetic content, the medium Whitaker used to publicise his views also hinted at the way things were to be in future. As later with the Grey Book, Whitaker did not choose to state his thoughts in a civil service memorandum, more than likely to be filed away to collect dust. Instead, he took his case to the public, one that was small but influential. The paper was published in *Administration*, the journal of the Institute of Public Administration. Whitaker had submitted the paper to Finance Minister, Gerard Sweetman, who gave his nod to publishing the article. Insignificant as this may seem, it was a key break with the Irish civil service's passion for anonymity.

A few days after Whitaker had submitted his paper to the Statistical Society, the government, on Sweetman's recommendation, appointed him Secretary of the Department of Finance. Looking back on it, Whitaker has referred to his appointment as 'a happy coincidence', but also as a source of inspiration: 'There was, I think I can say, this sense of mission about it.'[59]

A spur to action from another quarter occurred barely seven months after Whitaker assumed his new post. In January 1957, Seán Lemass gave his key economic speech on national production, outlining Fianna Fáil's proposals to deal with the ills of the economy. Reading of the Lemass Plan filled Whitaker with hope – a hope that someone could produce something better. He felt Lemass's speech was a simplistic and opportunistic appeal to people anxious about rising unemployment. But Whitaker's keen awareness of the political constraints on policy-making caused

42

him to welcome any new economic thinking by a key political figure. He may have regarded Lemass's remarks as amateurish from an economist's viewpoint, but it was encouraging that within Fianna Fáil, widely expected to return to office, there was at least one man who was thinking about government action to improve the Irish economy.

Whitaker was of the opinion that if Sweetman had remained as Finance Minister, he would have 'had both the energy and capacity to carry a thing like *Economic Development* through.'[60] It was unfortunate, said Whitaker, that having done 'all the unpopular things to get the balance of payments right and so on, out he [Sweetman] goes and leaves a clean sheet.'[61]

In late January 1957, Whitaker took a second important step towards *Economic Development* when he launched a far-reaching analysis of the Irish economy. In some respects this was a continuation of his earlier work, which he had completed primarily on his own, conversing informally with individuals such as Charles Murray of the Department of the Taoiseach, J.J. McElligott, the Governor of the Central Bank, and J.P. Beddy, the Chairman of the IDA. Whitaker described these conversations as 'all shades of support, from the pat on the back to really taking off their coats and doing something constructive.'[62]

Throughout the winter and early spring of 1957, Whitaker began to assemble a group of associates to assist him in preparing a detailed study of the entire Irish economy. Part of their task would be to recommend policies for economic improvement, an unprecedented step within the Irish Civil Service. Whitaker later commented, 'It was the first time officers of the Department of Finance were asked to do something constructive for the country.'[63] Charles Murray was formally appointed as co-ordinator, and Murray's recruitment demonstrated the importance of informal channels of communication in Ireland, where a relatively small population made it likely that most members of any profession would know each other personally. Senior civil servants were no exception. Although Murray and Whitaker worked in different government departments, their offices were just down the hall from each other, allowing frequent personal

43

contact. Murray had the rank of Principal, one grade below Assistant Secretary in the Department of the Taoiseach, and also served as an economic advisor to the Taoiseach. In keeping with his responsibility to stay fully informed of current economic affairs, Murray had access to a fund of information, making him ideally suited for the work Whitaker had in mind. Whitaker had already asked Murray for some help in preparing his paper on capital formation for the Statistical and Social Inquiry Society. It was only natural that the new Secretary turned to Murray when he needed a full-time co-ordinator for his study. Murray agreed to help in any way possible. He remained assigned to the Department of the Taoiseach but was relieved of his prior duties.

Whitaker also recruited Murray's assistant, Maurice Doyle, who was then attached to the Supply Division of the Department of Finance. In January 1957, Whitaker sent Doyle a list of fifty-six questions about agriculture. They were not casual queries but probing inquiries reflecting years of thought. Before Doyle had had a chance to answer more than a few of them, Whitaker summoned him to his office and announced that he had been relieved of his administrative duties and reassigned to work with Murray and Whitaker on the economic study. As the final step in the recruitment process, Whitaker wanted a five-man team to prepare the industrial sections of the study. Late in 1957, Whitaker had circulated a memorandum to the four Assistant Secretaries of the Finance Department. In this note, Whitaker briefly described the lines along which he had been working and what he hoped to prepare. The Secretary then asked each of his four assistants to nominate one or two men from his section to assist in preparing the part of the study relating to industry. From these recommendations, Whitaker chose five officials – S. Kissane, J. Dolan, M. Horgan, D. Lynch and T. Coffey – to research and draft the industry and tourism sections of *Economic Development*.

At the team's first meeting, Whitaker described what had already been done and how he hoped to utilise their talents. He made it clear from the outset that this project would involve considerable time, both official and personal, yet he could not relieve them of their regular duties. Whitaker requested rather than demanded their assistance, but all five agreed to help in any capacity. As one later recalled, 'I felt honoured to have been selected to participate in this study, and so I was more than willing to do anything that I could.'[64] Their reaction delighted Whitaker. 'I was glad to discover, when I tried to organise *Economic Development*, a very great response by the officers of the Department', he said later. 'They really wanted to co-operate, being given the chance to be in on something constructive, and they were prepared to work night and day.'[65] While it is unrealistic to envisage that a team of Irish civil servants worked sixteen hours a day, seven days a week like a group of New York investment bankers in the middle of a large merger, it was still a tribute to Dr Whitaker's leadership that his recruits were so eager to help.

Whitaker deliberately kept the project confined to the Department of Finance, except for the help of Murray from the Taoiseach's office. He had no intention of creating an inter-departmental group. Having spent years in the Irish government bureaucracy, he professed 'no belief at all in the virtues of committees but preferred a devoted team of collaborators.'[66] Another reason the study was kept within a single department was the limited use originally envisioned for the project. Whitaker and his staff had little inkling of the importance their work would later assume. As one member wrote, his enthusiasm 'sprang from a sense of personal involvement in a study which responsible public servants would consider worthwhile for its own sake and which held out, additionally, the strong possibility of positive follow-up action.'[67]

Throughout 1957 Whitaker's team worked hard on the project. Besides assigning tasks and doing general editing, Whitaker himself drafted the four opening chapters, chapter 12 and the concluding chapter. Murray co-ordinated much of the work, met often with Whitaker, and himself drafted chapters 9 and 10. Dr Brendan Menton also gave continuous help. Meanwhile, Maurice Doyle researched, outlined and drafted most of the sections on agriculture (chapters 5-8 and 11). Although the five officials assigned to the chapters on industry could not devote their full time to the study, they usually spent a few hours each day on it and often worked at home during the evening. Their individual assignments varied. A single individual might be responsible for an entire chapter, two might work on a section together, or all five might contribute. It is difficult to pinpoint who was responsible for each particular section because Whitaker held a meeting once a week to discuss progress and problems. If a team member desired assistance, he prepared a memorandum, circulated it and received advice at the next meeting.

This pattern of study continued until November 1957. At this time the five-man team drafted a series of comprehensive memoranda setting down their findings. Murray and Doyle edited these drafts and combined them with Doyle's agricultural sections. A complete draft was then circulated as the basis of lengthy discussions.

Two months earlier, in September 1957, the humourous magazine *Dublin Opinion* published a cartoon on its cover depicting Ireland as a woman asking a fortune teller if she had any future. Responding some years later to an interviewer's question as to when he first conceived the need for economic planning, Whitaker replied, 'As far as I remember, the immediate stimulus was seeing a cover of *Dublin Opinion*.'[68] Since Whitaker's survey of the Irish economy was partially completed by then, this event was more likely to have reinforced his belief that the on-going work was important.

Whitaker told Fianna Fáil's Minister for Finance, James Ryan, of his study for the first time just before Christmas. Ryan offered his immediate support. At Ryan's prodding, the government instructed other departments to help Whitaker complete his study. Intense inter-departmental rivalry would have doomed any request for co-operation if Whitaker had proceeded on his own. But the government's directive left departmental chiefs little choice. Access to other departments put specialised information and individual expertise at the service of the team from Finance. Doyle and Murray utilised the Department of Agriculture's statistical studies, unavailable elsewhere. Doyle had written the first draft of his sections on agriculture, and Whitaker and Murray had jotted notes in the margins. After Doyle had revised his draft incorporating Whitaker's and Murray's comments, he sent the revised version to the Department of Agriculture for further suggestions. Doyle then rewrote the agricultural sections once more in the light of these observations. Unlike the sections on agriculture, those dealing with industry had been practically completed by the time Whitaker first spoke with Ryan. Consequently, Whitaker's task-force consulted the Department of Industry and Commerce only sporadically. Using information obtained from these inter-departmental discussions, the team drew up a 'first edition' of *Economic Development* in May 1958. A limited edition of fifty copies was circulated to other government departments. After receiving their comments, Whitaker and his staff prepared a second edition in July 1958.

This edition, circulated in November, included some minor alterations as a result of continuing talks with other departments. Whitaker himself spoke to senior civil servants of departments such as Agriculture, Industry and Commerce, Lands and Education. According to Charles Murray, 'there was occasional resentment but no more difficulty than usual in dealing with other departments.'[69] Understandably, these departments did not like the intrusion into what they considered their private bailiwick. Their displeasure grew even more acute at the favourable publicity that soon cast a flattering spotlight on the Department of Finance.

Subsequent editions like the November version did not materially differ from the first version in May, but the revisions did have one important effect. Whitaker and his associates received advice and information from other government departments, but it was the Finance Department whose officials decided what should be added or deleted. As a result, Whitaker's Department further consolidated its position as first among equals. Moreover, this project set an important precedent for Finance's primary − some would argue sole − responsibility in the formulation of national economic programmes. While Whitaker and his team made some changes in the Grey Book between May and November 1958, they spent most of their time drafting a shorter policy statement for the government based on *Economic Development*.

ADOPTION AND PUBLICATION OF THE WHITAKER PLAN

Government Approval

Whitaker had begun work on his economic study in January 1957. James Ryan, the Fianna Fáil Finance Minister, took office on 20 March but did not hear of Whitaker's work until almost nine months later. Throughout 1957,Whitaker and Ryan held frequent discussions during which, Ryan has said, Whitaker 'mentioned economic planning.'[70] Whitaker corroborates this account; he told Ryan only 'vague details of the project' before the December meeting.[71] A few days before Christmas 1957, Ryan received an unexpected present. Just as their regular weekly meeting of 12 December was ending, Whitaker told Ryan of his economic study. He handed the Minister a memorandum broadly outlining *Economic Development*, and asked him to read it. According to Whitaker, this December meeting was the first time he 'felt able to define the project with exactness and to give the whole scope of something well conceived and planned already.'[72]

The relationship between Whitaker and Ryan was unusual. In an interview in August 1986, Whitaker recalls:

> Not only was he [Ryan] very shrewd and quick, but he had great courage politically and also had the good sense to leave technical things to the technocrats and to concern himself with what was politically viable. In many ways he was the ideal minister. He was available for the crucial decisions and applied his very shrewd mind to them very well indeed. He was decisive, despite his bluff, country manner. This was a sort of pose. I found my period with him a most co-operative one. He was a sort of political father-figure who provided a screen for you to advance along the other front.[73]

Whitaker reveals his own shrewdness in recognising the need for a senior civil servant and minister to complement each other.

Ryan reacted favourably to Whitaker's study. At Ryan's suggestion, Whitaker prepared a memorandum summarising their conversation of 12 December, and explaining his proposals. Following customary procedure, the Minister for Finance circulated what later became known as the 'Whitaker Memorandum', to all Cabinet members so that this matter could be discussed at the next weekly meeting, scheduled for 17 December.

The 'Whitaker Memorandum' was a condensed version of his longer study. It contained a brief outline of the state of the Irish economy, followed by a general statement of principles for improving that economy and several specific proposals to promote economic development. In his memorandum, Whitaker stressed the importance of deciding which of the so-called 'unproductive investments', such as hospitals, roads, government houses and schools, could be curtailed to free resources for 'productive' investment. Whitaker followed this recommendation with five reasons why such a study was urgently needed. He cited the prevailing mood of despondency about the country's future, the need for a coherent overall programme rather than a series of individual policies, and the increased unemployment which would soon result from a slowing down in house construction. He also mentioned the balance of payments problem and the need to prepare for the upcoming meeting with a delegation from the World Bank. Whitaker went on to urge the establishment of reasonable targets for economic growth and to recommend that work on the study be continued under the direction of a single person, namely Whitaker, in the Department of Finance. In conclusion, Whitaker asked the government to grant two requests: approval to complete the project and free access to other departments for information.

On 17 December 1957, the ministers assembled in Government Buildings on Merrion Street for one of their twice-weekly meetings. The agenda included a discussion of Whitaker's proposals. Three individuals at this meeting had a crucial say in all Cabinet decisions: the Minister for Finance, James Ryan, the Minister for Industry and Commerce, Seán Lemass, and the Taoiseach, Éamon de Valera. A fourth, Seán MacEntee, carried substantial if extremely conservative weight in government deliberations.

The Minister for Finance was the link between Whitaker and the government. Dr Ryan gave him more than support. He put forward Whitaker's proposals to his government colleagues without delay, without changes, and without hiding the source. As a leading Irish economist, Professor Patrick Lynch, was later to explain, 'Dr. Ryan knew the quality of Dr. Whitaker's mind and had the good sense to accept Whitaker's proposals when a less appreciative Minister, or a more timid one, might have been afraid to break with convention about the anonymity of the Irish civil servant.'[74] A future Taoiseach, Jack Lynch, was present at this Cabinet meeting. His recollection was that Jim Ryan was not particularly enthusiastic about the plan, but stressed 'that Ryan was not too enthusiastic about anything'.[75] Ryan's rugged manner often obscured his acute political judgment. He was shrewd enough to realise that economic problems had ousted the second coalition government in early 1957 and that, after ten months in office, Fianna Fáil was coming under increasing attack for its failure to deal effectively with those same problems. As early as May 1957, during the budget debate, Ryan argued (in a speech Dr Whitaker wrote for the Fianna Fáil Minister): 'The policies of the past, though successful in some directions, have not so far given us what we want. . . . Further progress on a worthwhile scale calls for comprehensive review of our economic policy'.[76]

The Taoiseach, Éamon de Valera, carried the most weight in the decision-making process. As head of the government and of Fianna Fáil, he had to approve all major political announcements. His objection alone would be enough to doom the entire proposal. At seventy-six and almost blind, de Valera still maintained absolute party discipline. No minister or group of ministers could force him to accept a policy which he found fatally flawed. As one Fine Gael member of parliament commented, 'Of course, Dev would not have done it wantonly, only if he, and he alone, thought it necessary'.[77] While he regarded economic development as relevant and supported Lemass's industrialisation policy, it did not rank high on his list of priorities. In his famous St Patrick's Day speech of 1943, he had proclaimed:

> The Ireland which we have dreamed of would be the home of a people who valued material wealth only as the basis for right living, of a people who were satisfied with frugal things of the spirit, a land whose

countryside would be bright with cosy homesteads, whose fields and villages would be joyous with the sounds of industry, with the romping of sturdy children, the contests of athletic youths, the laughter of comely maidens, whose firesides would be forums for the wisdom of old age. It would, in a word, be the home of people living the life that God desires that men should live.[78]

In his definition of the 'life that God desires', de Valera uses the word industry only in the context of work in fields and villages. There is no mention whatever of towns or cities, and no reference to industry in the sense that the rest of Europe would understand. The 'frugal things of the spirit' are unquestionably of great value. Unfortunately for Ireland, they were not the foundation on which the great modern economies had already been built by the time of the St Patrick's Day speech.

An incident a few years after adoption of the 1958 Plan reveals much about de Valera's attitude. Meeting Whitaker at a cocktail party, the Taoiseach complimented him on the plan he had constructed for the Irish economy, adding in Irish, 'Ach tá rudaí eile níos tábhachtaí' (But there are more important things.)[79] De Valera's idea was that Ireland would produce and consume whatever it needed, exporting only what was necessary to obtain foreign exchange. This policy failed to recognise the limitations of both country and climate or to capitalise on the advantages of being on the edge of one of the biggest world markets. As Whitaker put it in 1967:

To expect laissez-faire to solve our problems is like seeking a return to the eighteenth-century sedan chair as a solution to the problems caused by the motor car. To plan or not to plan is not the question of our time. The real issue is the achievement of the required degree of planning and its development and improvement.[80]

At the government meeting on 17 December, de Valera endorsed Whitaker's study but suggested that it was merely a continuation of long-established policy. Twelve years after this meeting, de Valera still claimed that Whitaker had proposed nothing new. We set out those policies in 1926 at the formation of Fianna Fáil,'[81] de Valera stated. In fact, the 1926 manifesto included calls for reunification, revival of the Irish language and keeping as many people as possible working on the land. Other elements of the early Fianna Fáil economic platform included self-sufficiency in wheat and other products, indiscriminate industrial protectionism and 'Irish-only' ownership of new industry. It was a tribute to de Valera's political genius that he could claim the 1958 Whitaker plan was a continuation of the party's founding principles in 1926. *Economic Development* provided de Valera and his Fianna Fáil party an escape hatch from those 1926 policies which had been tried and found wanting. As an astute politician, de Valera recognised this fact, gave his assent to Whitaker's plan and still claimed with his legendary verbal sleight-of-hand that nothing had changed (English Prime Minister Lloyd George once quipped that arguing with de Valera was like trying to pick up mercury with a fork). Years later Whitaker described de Valera and his relationship with Lemass as follows:

> First of all one must see that Dev recognised, through the eminence he gave to Lemass, the deficiency in his own viewpoint. De Valera was supplementing his idealistic view of things by a practical go-getter person in Lemass. Dev was still Taoiseach when they decided to publish this piece of official advice, something never heard of before and strongly resisted by Seán MacEntee at the time. One is left thinking that it was his political instinct — it was a way out, a brilliant way out from being imprisoned in the old policies. Dev presumably had the perception to see that change was necessary.[82]

Lemass was the third key figure in the Cabinet. His importance is harder to evaluate since in many ways he was the *de facto* Taoiseach, although technically de Valera was still in charge. Ken Whitaker had the following view:

> I must say it was a very pleasant surprise when the Fianna Fáil government, committed so much to self-sufficiency and protection, abandoned it all so readily. There is no doubt that Lemass was the great moving dynamic spirit in all of this. There was grudging acquiescence, or recognition granted, that without Lemass's drive and also probably without de Valera's benevolent blessing, change would not have come about nearly as quickly.

As Whitaker was to say later,

> Lemass was a pragmatic nationalist, and I put the emphasis on the two words. He was a nationalist in the sense of wanting to see Ireland have a respectable place in the world, but I don't think he was opposed to Dev's traditionalist outlook. He simply had some impatience with it in so far as it might be a hindrance to change, the change he wanted. He didn't have a programme of cultural change. His aim, as indeed my own, was focussed on improving the economic and social scene.[83]

Although Irish governments (like their British counterparts) often give the impression of unanimity even while disagreeing violently in private, the Cabinet suffered no serious division over the 'Whitaker Memorandum'. Even Seán MacEntee, who would later oppose publication of *Economic Development* under Whitaker's name, agreed with the government's approval of Whitaker's study because he felt that 'all the wheels should be put in gear.'[84] Apart from Lemass, few Irish politicians had any interest in economics, and agreement is easier when potential dissenters do not consider the issue salient. As John Healy, then Ireland's leading political newspaper columnist, speculated: 'I think it is a myth to even think of a huddle of Fianna Fáil deputies solemnly considering the implications of the Whitaker "Grey Paper" . . . the poor whores, most of them still don't know what GNP means and "indices" looks like a dirty word.'[85] So out of a combination of indifference and astuteness, the government affirmed Whitaker's proposals without opposition.

For a meeting that effectively fired the first shot in Ireland's economic revolution, the 17 December gathering had all the immediate impact of a pop-gun. Maurice Moynihan (then Secretary to the Government and later Governor of the Central Bank) sent a memorandum to Finance and all other government departments and State organisations for information. After discussing 'the working-out of an integrated programme of national development', the government directed the Minister for Finance, James Ryan, to 'approve the proposals, submitted to him in the minute, for the preparation of a study.'[86] When the Fianna Fáil Cabinet adjourned its meeting, few, if any, realised the long-term importance of the action they had taken.

On 18 December, the day after the crucial government meeting, Whitaker wrote personally and confidentially to the heads of the other departments. He informed them of the decision to allow him access and requested their co-operation and support. In the months to come, men and women throughout the civil service would become involved in one of the most exciting projects they had ever tackled. Whitaker went to great lengths to stress the project's co-operative nature and the need for everyone's wholehearted support. The response he received was almost unanimously positive. This may have stemmed in part from the general realisation that the outlook for the country was dismal. Whatever the reason for it, this co-operation is very evident in the speed with which things progressed. Whitaker finished a first draft of the first two chapters by 3 January 1958, setting the tone and the direction for the entire report. By 1 January, he was able to dispatch a first draft of chapter 3, on financial and monetary policy, to his predecessor, J.J. McElligott, who had been the first-ranking civil servant in the Finance Department for more than thirty years. Whitaker wanted his old boss's views. 'Nobody else has seen the draft – or will see it – until I hear from you',[87] Whitaker wrote. According to Ronan Fanning, 'Others who played a significant part in the process of consultation were M.D. McCarthy (the head of the Central Statistics Office) and the three economists then serving on the Capital Investment Advisory Committee – Carter, Lynch and Ryan.'[88] Charles Carter was an English economist and former editor of the *Economic Journal* while Patrick Lynch taught economics at University College, Dublin and W.J. Louden Ryan did the same at Trinity College, Dublin. On 9 May a proof copy was prepared and a printed copy delivered to the government on 29 May. The government requested that it be circulated to all departments and state-sponsored bodies. The Minister for Finance was to submit a revised draft incorporating any necessary revisions on 1 July.

However, the government still had to decide what to do with *Economic Development*. First they set up a committee to transform *Economic Development* into an official government White Paper. Second, the government determined that not only would

Economic Development be published, but it would be published under Whitaker's name.

The Lemass Committee

In the early summer of 1958, the government had been unsure how they should deal with Whitaker's economic proposals. Some wanted his paper published immediately, while others wanted further study before publishing anything. Finally, on 22 July 1958, Lemass convinced the government to set up a committee to prepare a shorter White Paper extracted from *Economic Development*. The point of doing this was to show that the recommendations were official government policy, not merely proposals from the bureaucracy. The committee consisted of the ministers concerned with economic affairs: Chairman Seán Lemass (Industry and Commerce), James Ryan (Finance), Erskine Childers (Lands) and Patrick Smith (Agriculture). Parallelling the ministers' committee was an inter-departmental civil service group comprised of the respective secretaries and co-ordinated by Charles Murray.

The four government ministers supervised the drafting of the White Paper by Charles Murray. The committee met about every two weeks to decide what changes if any, should be made in Murray's drafts, which were in fact extracts from Whitaker's report. The elected officials found some parts of *Economic Development* politically sensitive. For example, Whitaker had written, 'The policies hitherto followed, though given a fair trial, have not resulted in a viable economy.'[89] But many of the Fianna Fáil ministers on the Lemass committee had formulated and implemented previous Irish economic policy, so they understandably rejected this statement in the White Paper.

The Decision to Publish

In the early days of working on *Economic Development*, Whitaker had thought of publishing the work privately. As a colleague put it, 'Ken saw no reason why all this information should just collect dust in the basement of some government building'.[99] Whitaker had previously written articles on economic issues which were approved for publication by the then government minister and published in *Administration*, the journal of the Dublin-based Institute for Public Administration. Initially he had envisaged the same forum for a book-length study. On one afternoon in 1957, he even discussed the idea with Tom Barrington, then head of the Institute of Public Administration, over drinks in Dublin's Shelbourne Hotel. Whitaker briefly described his study and asked Barrington about the possibility of publishing it with government approval as an Institute-sponsored book. Barrington expressed interest, but no further discussion ever took place.

The Fianna Fáil government finally agreed to publish the study but were divided over precisely how to arrange this. One possibility was to bring out the report as an anonymous document. Alternatively, the study could be (and was) published with reference to Dr Whitaker as the principal author of the work. This trivial-seeming decision involved weighty issues of precedent, government policy, credit for work, political considerations and ministerial responsibility. Lemass and Ryan both felt Whitaker's name should be included in the document, while Seán MacEntee vigorously opposed any mention of the author. Whitaker agreed with Lemass and Ryan: 'It was important, that the public should see what I had produced because it was generally hopeful about the future of the economy. Also, the government recognised the psychological importance of showing that my study was not a political gimmick. Producing an economic programme was different from producing a platform for an election.'[91] Finance Minister Ryan was the key player who insisted that *Economic Development* be published under Whitaker's name. He appreciated the considerable time and energy that Whitaker's team of civil servants had spent on the project and he did not want those efforts to go unnoticed. As Ryan himself put it, 'The civil service never gets the credit it deserves.'[92] Ryan perhaps had other motives besides altruism. Publishing *Economic Development* under Whitaker's name would be an astute political move. Ryan perhaps would receive credit for nourishing genius, while at the same time undermining part of the opposition with the work of one of their own appointees, Dr Whitaker.

Seán Lemass agreed with Ryan that Whitaker's name should

be linked with the report. 'Its publication as an anonymous government publication would give it political aspects which we did not want,' he said. 'The association with the name of a non-political civil servant would help to get its acceptance over political boundaries. . . . It was a deliberate decision, part of our effort to get economic development away from party political tags.'[93] Seán MacEntee stubbornly opposed publication of the study under the name of a civil servant. He felt that such a publication would sanction displacement of ministerial responsibility and prerogative and even prepared a memorandum to that effect. MacEntee proposed releasing *Economic Development* as a government document, not as a civil servant's study,'[94] but the view of Ryan and Lemass prevailed.

Publication of 'Programme for Economic Expansion' and 'Economic Development'

Both the White Paper and what came to be known as the Grey Book were published in November of 1958 even though the Grey Book had been completed six months earlier. The White Paper, which had been taken to the meeting of the World Bank the previous month, appeared as an official government document. On Tuesday, 11 November 1958, each member of both houses of the Oireachtas received a copy of the White Paper entitled: *Programme for Economic Expansion*. Éamon de Valera invited Whitaker to attend the parliamentary session and personally congratulated him. The deputies in the Dáil were offered no formal resolution or debate. Referring to the months of preparation that had gone into the White Paper and *Economic Development*, Ken Whitaker recalled:

> It was a kind of dawn in which it was bliss to be alive. There were a few small teams working on different aspects, such as industry and tourism. We worked into the night and were early to work, with real enthusiasm, the next morning. We were refreshed by our release from a purely negative role and the feeling that we were doing something constructive and worthwhile.[95]

Following publication of the White Paper, front-page synopses of it appeared in all three Dublin newspapers. Editorial comment varied. The Fianna Fáil-oriented *Irish Press* praised the event, trumpeting: 'The government in its recent White Paper on economic development has shown that it is determined to approach the task of agricultural and industrial expansion in a comprehensive way.'[96] The independent but conservative *Irish Times* — which modelled itself on the *Times* of London — reacted without enthusiasm one way or another: 'For the moment, it is sufficient that there is nothing basically new in the plan.'[97] The Fine Gael-leaning *Irish Independent* did not give any editorial review of the White Paper.

Eleven days later, on Saturday 21 November, the goverment issued Whitaker's *Economic Development* with the grey cover that gave the report its nickname. On the title page appeared the words: 'This study of national development problems and opportunities was prepared by the Secretary of the Department of Finance, with the cooperation of others in, or connected with, the public service.'[98] Unlike the White Paper, the book was not presented to deputies or senators. Six copies of the document were placed in the library of the Oireachtas, the normal method of circulating official documents to elected representatives. Reaction to *Economic Development* was also in sharp contrast to the publicity surrounding the White Paper. It was published with so little fuss that two of the three national dailies ignored it completely, while the third confined itself to quoting from the proposal put to the government in December 1957, giving no information whatever about the contents of the document.

It was only some days later that newspapers gave any notice to *Economic Development*. The *Irish Press* dismissed it with faint praise, calling the book 'a most useful addition to the literature on national economics.'[99] But the *Irish Times* recognised the far-reaching potential of the Grey Book, calling it 'in its implication almost revolutionary.'[100] The 26 November edition of the newspaper noted three important aspects of the study, all of which became more apparent in later years. First, Whitaker emerged as 'a singularly independent, farsighted, and progressive civil servant.'[101] Second, the *Irish Times* applauded the govern ment's publication of the original draft, 'so that all may see exactly where the discrepancies are, and to what extent expediency, or political motives, may have come into play.'[102] Third, the book broke new ground in the 'transfer of responsibility for all economic planning to the Department of Finance.'[103] The *Irish Times* went on to warn that 'war will rage over the government's five-year plan . . . when it comes before Dáil Éireann.'[104] In fact, government reaction to the book was notable mainly because of its absence. Neither house of the Oireachtas formally debated or otherwise discussed in detail the White Paper or Grey Book. Foreshadowing the Grey Book's publication, Éamon de Valera said on 30 October 1958:

> Before questions, I was pointing out that as a result of a very comprehensive survey which had been made of the whole field of the economy and a very thorough study based on that survey, the government had come to a decision on a programme envisioning public capital expenditure on an average of about £44,000,000 yearly. I do not think it would be desirable to go into this matter piecemeal. The Programme will be published in a White Paper soon. If the Dáil requires to discuss it, an opportunity for doing that can be given.[105]

No such requirement made itself felt. In response to one question from Noel Browne, James Ryan replied: '*Economic Development* was published to make available the information assembled and co-ordinated in it and to stimulate interest in the subject of national development.'[106] Seán Lemass offered one explanation of the Dáil's silence on the subject. 'The debate was more in the country than in the Dáil,' said Lemass. 'There was no desire to have a Dáil debate on fundamentals of planning because Opposition parties did not want to contribute to the support of a government document, and besides government is always pressed for time in the Dáil.'[107]

SUMMARY OF *ECONOMIC DEVELOPMENT*

In a telling paragraph in *Economic Development*, Whitaker quotes from the Bishop of Clonfert, Most Rev Dr Philbin: 'We seem to have relaxed our patriotic energies just at the time when there was most need to mobilise them. Although our enterprise in purely spiritual fields has never been greater, we have shown little initiative or organisational ability in agriculture and industry and commerce.'[108] *Economic Development* revealed Ireland's economic position in a harsh but honest light: the country had the lowest income *per capita* in Western Europe, sluggish GNP growth, little entrepreneurial activity and low levels of savings and private capital investment. As both cause and effect of these failings, Ireland was the only country in Western Europe with a declining population. Whitaker wanted the private sector, either Irish or foreign, to be the principal source of new enterprises. The State would provide some extra development assistance, a contribution of £44 million pounds over five years. An early 'supply-sider', Whitaker urged lowering individual and corporate taxes to encourage savings and investment in factories. He also hoped that banks and insurance companies would join the State in providing loans for industry through the Industrial Credit Corporation and to agriculture through the Agricultural Credit Corporation. The Grey Book exhorted Irish agriculture to produce goods at prices competitive enough to export. Government assistance should not take the form of price supports or guarantees, but should strive to lower costs by such means as subsidies to encourage greater use of fertilizers. In a departure from the traditional Fianna Fáil policy, Whitaker believed that beef, rather than tillage crops and dairy production, was the key to agricultural growth. As for manufacturing, Whitaker argued that the government should encourage industries which would be competitive in the world markets and provide a continuing source of employment at home. One way of doing this, Whitaker argued, was to encourage foreign investment in Ireland:

> We can no longer rely for industrial development on extensive tariff and quota protection. Foreign industrialists will bring skills and techniques we need, and continuous and widespread publicity abroad is essential to attract them. If foreign industrial investment does not rapidly increase, a more radical removal of statutory restrictions on such investments should take place.[109]

Whitaker's vision heralded the major economic achievement of the sixties. The main thrust of *Economic Development*, both in terms of the amount of detail in the report and of the impact it had on the country's self-confidence, was the need for industrial investment and expansion. Whitaker outlined two ways to attract multinational corporations: removing restrictions and giving incentives for foreign firms to establish factories in Ireland. The Control of Manufacturers Acts of 1932 and 1934 required, or tried to require, that any new manufacturing company in Ireland was to be controlled by Irish nationals. Whitaker wrote that the country could no longer 'afford to retain the controls we have been exercising against foreign participation in the ownership of Irish industries',[110] and went on to praise legislation in 1958 which amended, in certain respects, the 1932 and 1934 Control of Manufacturers Acts. Revoking some of these prior restraints was a major reversal of past Fianna Fáil policy. The party had long followed a policy of protectionism and self-sufficiency. Besides opening up the economy, *Economic Development* proposed specific incentives to attract direct foreign investment. Whitaker recommended that the Industrial Development Authority should enlarge its staff, particularly in North America, to intensify its efforts to attract outside investors to Ireland. He further proposed increasing the capital available for outright industrial grants. The Grey Book contained only one macroeconomic goal, which Whitaker left vaguely defined. Citing the one per cent annual GNP growth rate between 1949 and 1956, Whitaker suggested that 'there is good reason to believe that, if the proposals were adopted, the rate of increase in the volume of gross national product could, in time, be doubled.'[111] Whitaker was careful not to specify what time period was involved.

White Paper: Political Genuflections

The White Paper represented the formal political endorsement of all the work done by Whitaker and his team. It gave his economic study both muscle and endurance. Because the White Paper was only fifty pages long, it necessarily eliminated much of the economic background in the 250 page Grey Book. A further difference between the two documents was the period of time covered in each one. The Grey Book considered fiscal years 1958/9 to 1962/3, but because of the delay in drafting, the White Paper covered the fiscal years 1959/60 through 1963/4. The White Paper's cost estimate for its development proposals was somewhat higher than those of the Grey Book. And unlike *Economic Development*, which was vague on the goal for growth in GNP, the White Paper confidently predicted a two per cent annual increase in national income in each of the coming five years.

The White Paper diverged from the Grey Book in more fundamental ways. It modified some salient points which had been part of Whitaker's original thinking, but which the committee saw as politically controversial. One such modification related to the support of tillage crops such as wheat, barley, and sugarbeets. While the Grey Book encouraged capital-intensive cattle production as a substitute, the White Paper made political genuflections to the traditional Fianna Fáil policy of supporting labour-intensive tillage farming, 'Although the total area under tillage is only a relatively small proportion of the total acreage of agricultural land, it is important that the tillage area be at least maintained,' the White Paper stated.[112] A second significant difference concerned price supports for certain agricultural products. The Grey Book proposed abandoning supports for barley, whereas the White Paper left the question open. Third, the White Paper announced that the government had decided to introduce legislation to establish a permanent state body (Córas Tráchtála Teo) to promote exports, especially to North America. *Economic Development* had not mentioned this. Fourth, the White Paper called for construction of a nitrogen fertilizer plant in Ireland while *Economic Development* favoured accepting low-price fertilizer from abroad. Finally, the White Paper omitted Whitaker's suggestion that new industries should be located at or near large urban centres. The impetus for this decision doubtless was Fianna Fáil's desire not to alienate its traditional support in rural areas. The Grey Book's argument about the higher costs associated with rural-based factories would not have endeared the party to much of its traditional electorate.

Economic Development was a study of the economy, fleshed out with suggestions for direction and policy. Because it was intended as a basis for government policy, it had to be more defined, more precise and more detailed. The White Paper, by contrast, was not a study; it was a statement of policy on which the government would in due course be judged by the electorate. Consequently, political considerations had to be worked into the programme, influencing in some ways the Grey Book's economic framework. The White Paper nevertheless sought to convey the basic structure of what was set out in *Economic Development.*

During the five years that followed publication of the 1958 White Paper, GNP grew by over four per cent per year, twice the targeted growth. Unemployment dropped by one-third, emigration fell to less than half of its 1954–61 level, the population began to rise again, and the volume of national investment almost doubled.

CONCLUSION

With world trade investment flourishing in the early sixties, it is likely that some degree of economic recovery, however, would have occurred in Ireland with or without the recommendations outlined in the Whitaker Plan. Psychological recovery might have been more elusive without *Economic Development.* Instead of the crushing sense of gloom that pervaded Ireland during the 1957/8 recession, Whitaker offered a vision of hope.

The Grey Book contained no radical approaches. Grants to new industries and tax reliefs for manufactured exports had already become part of Irish economic policy. Whitaker did not transform Ireland: its most intractable problems, such as unemployment and relatively low national income, have not yet been solved. But the stagnant Irish economy did move forward. The government had set a goal of doubling the national rate of growth, and, to almost everyone's surprise, this goal not only was achieved but was surpassed. The country was far better off when Whitaker retired as Finance Secretary in 1969 than when he took office in 1956. Few members of the Irish political élite can honestly make that claim.

STATISTICAL PROFILE OF THE IRISH ECONOMY
1956, 1969

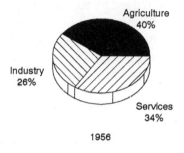 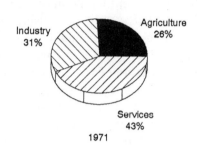

Sectoral Employment Shares

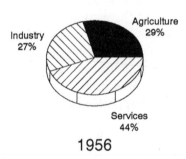 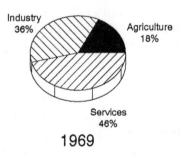

National Income: Sectoral Shares

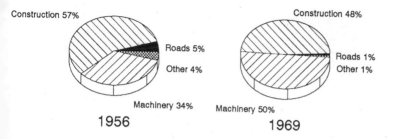

Construction 57%
Roads 5%
Other 4%
Machinery 34%
1956

Construction 48%
Roads 1%
Other 1%
Machinery 50%
1969

Investment by Type

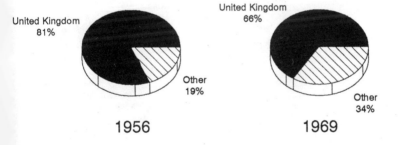

United Kingdom 81%
Other 19%
1956

United Kingdom 66%
Other 34%
1969

Exports Destination

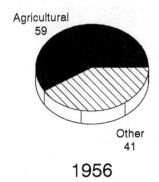

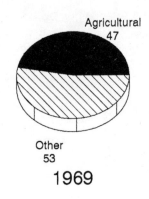

Exports Composition

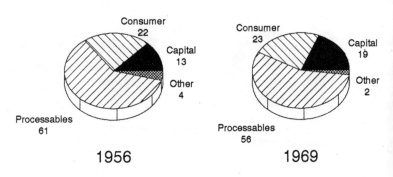

Imports Composition

Sources:
Census of Population, 1956 and 1971.
National Income and Expenditure, 1958 and 1971.
Statistical Abstracts, 1958 and 1971.

IRELAND'S TURNAROUND
NOTES

1. Interview of Dr T.K. Whitaker with Bruce Arnold in August 1986. The author gratefully acknowledges the assistance of Bruce Arnold in the research and writing of this article. I am also indebted to Professors Walter F. Murphy and Cyril Black of Princeton University for grants from the National Science Foundation and the Woodrow Wilson School of Public and International Affairs.
2. Interview of Dr T.K. Whitaker with Bruce Arnold in August 1986.
3. Kerby Miller, *Emigrants and Exiles: Ireland and the Irish Exodus to North America* (New York, 1985), p. 429.
4. *Ibid.*, p. 428.
5. Joel Mokyr, *Why Ireland Starved: A Quantitative and Analytical History of the Irish Economy* (London, 1985), pp. 146-7.
6. Interview of Gerard Sweetman with the author on 6 August 1969.
7. Ronan Fanning, *The Irish Department of Finance 1922-1958* (Dublin, 1978) — hereafter cited as Fanning — p. 504.
8. Interview of T.K. Whitaker with Bruce Arnold in August 1986.
9. *Ibid.*
10. *Ibid.*
11. US Department of State, *The European Recovery Program, Country Studies*, Chapter VIII — Ireland, April 1948. Reprinted in *The European Recovery Programme: Basic Documents and Background Information*, P. No. 8792 (Dublin, 1949), p. 133.
12. James Meenan, *The Irish Economy Since 1922* (Liverpool, 1970), p. 390.
13. Interview of T.K. Whitaker with Bruce Arnold in August 1986.
14. Interview of T.K. Whitaker with the author on 2 September 1969.
15. *Blueprint for Prosperity* (Dublin, 1953), p. 5.
16. *Ibid.*, p. 14.
17. Lemass's son-in-law and future Taoiseach, Charles J. Haughey recalled that his father-in-law did a great deal of reading during the 1954-57 period in opposition, expressly in the area of economics. One of Haughey's jobs on Mondays was to go out to the bookstore and buy certain books that Lemass had read about in the newspaper over the weekend (Interview of Charles J. Haughey with the author on 17 June 1986).
18. Interview of Seán F. Lemass with the author on 14 August 1969.
19. The *Irish Times*, 12 October 1955, page 1 to supplement.
20. Interview of Seán Lemass with the author on 14 August 1969.
21. Questionnaire sent by author to Noel Lemass and reply dated 15 January 1969.
22. Questionnaire sent by author to Fianna Fáil minister who requested to remain anonymous.

67

23. *The Policy for Production* (Dublin, 1956), p. 1.
24. *Ibid.*, p. 5.
25. Interview of Patrick Lynch with the author on 3 September 1969.
26. Alexis FitzGerald had been instrumental in setting up the Industrial Development Authority during the first coalition government 1948–51 and convincing Seán Lemass not to disband it when Fianna Fáil returned to government in 1951. A true Renaissance man, FitzGerald lectured for over twenty years in economics and commercial law at University College Dublin while at the same time building up the largest law firm in Ireland.
27. Interview of John A. Costello with the author on 15 July 1970.
28. The *Irish Times*, 8 October 1956, p. 1.
29. The *Irish Times*, 18 January 1957, p. 1.
30. *Ibid.*
31. *Ibid.*
32. *Ibid.*
33. *Ibid.*
34. Fanning, p. 449.
35. Letter dated 5 February 1969 from Gerard Sweetman to the author. Gerard Sweetman's appointment as Finance Minister had been greeted with scorn in many circles. Patrick McGilligan, an extremely able Fine Gael Finance Minister from 1948–51, had turned down Costello's offer of the Finance portfolio in the second coalition, as had John O'Donovan, formerly a high-ranking civil servant in the Finance Department. Far down on his list of candidates, Costello turned to the dapper Gerard Sweetman, a country lawyer from outside Dublin whose prior financial experience, his critics sniped, went no further than filing legal paper for bankruptcy proceedings. As one detractor, John O'Donovan, put it: 'When Sweetman took office he knew nothing, after six months he thought he knew everything.' (Interview of John O'Donovan with the author on 22 August 1973).
36. The Republican Party's decision to topple Costello prevented the surfacing of an internal split that might otherwise have brought down the second coalition. On Friday evening, 25 January 1957, Fine Gael Cabinet members met in the Department of Education office of party leader, Richard Mulcahy, to discuss the upcoming budget. When Finance Minister Sweetman announced his intention to cut off food subsidies four members of the Fine Gael élite, Liam Cosgrave (Minister for External Affairs), Tom O'Higgins (Minister for Health), Patrick McGilligan (Attorney General) and John O'Donovan (Parliamentary Secretary to the Government), threatened to resign. Even former Minister for Industry and Commerce, Dan Morrisey, whom Sweetman had brought along to support his position, remarked that the Fine Gael

dissidents had made up their minds not to accept more of Sweetman's proposals. As a pale Richard Mulcahy adjourned the meeting without a vote on the food subsidy question, one minister said he expected to see Sweetman's resignation in the Sunday paper. Others felt Sweetman would refuse to leave office, and the ensuing resignations would precipitate a general election.

But the Clann's defection prevented both wings from resigning. Instead of voting on the food subsidies question, the Fine Gael élite had to decide whether they should try to remain in office as a minority government or go to the country. At this decisive vote senior Fine Gael members (Prime Minister Costello, Agriculture Minister Dillon, Attorney General McGilligan, and Education Minister Mulcahy) opted for an immediate general election while younger men (e.g. Foreign Minister Liam Cosgrave, Local Government Minister Patrick O'Donnell and Health Minister T.F. O'Higgins) voted to stay on. There was speculation that the older Fine Gael men were weary of the turbulent two-and-a-half years in office and welcomed the return to their private professions, which for many was law. Losses in the next four general elections (which resulted in Fine Gael's exclusion from office for sixteen years) may have caused senior Fine Gael members to regret this decision. Interview of John O'Donovan with the author on 22 August 1973.

37. Interview of Seán F. Lemass with the author on 14 August 1969.
38. Peter Mair, 'Policy Competition', in *How Ireland Voted* (Dublin, 1987), p. 43.
39. The *Irish Times*, 26 February 1953, p. 1.
40. Interview of James Ryan with the author on 20 August 1969.
41. The *Irish Times*, 28 February 1957, p. 1.
42. Mair, p. 39.
43. Provisional United Trade Union Organisation, *Planning Full Employment* (Dublin, 1956). Document prepared by Dónal Nevin who was Research Officer for Irish Congress of Trade Unions, for a special conference of trade union representatives in Dublin on 3 Dec 1956.
44. The *Irish Times*, 26 February 1957, p. 4.
45. Letter of Seán F. Lemass to the author dated 12 February 1969.
46. Interview of T.K. Whitaker with Bruce Arnold in August 1986.
47. Fanning, p. 601.
48. *Economic Development* (Dublin, 1958), p. 2.
49. Source wishes to remain anonymous, letter to the author dated 3 March 1969.
50. Interview with the author. Source wishes to remain anonymous.
51. *Economic Development*, p. 5.
52. *Ibid.*, p. 228.

53. Interview of W.J. Louden Ryan with the author on 1 September 1969.
54. W.J.L. Ryan and M. O'Donoghue, 'The Republic of Ireland', reprinted in *Papers on Regional Development*, p. 90.
55. *Economic Development*, p. 207.
56. Interview of T.K. Whitaker with the author on 2 September 1969.
57. Interview of T.K. Whitaker with Bruce Arnold in August 1986.
58. Paper read to the Statistical and Social Inquiry Society of Ireland in May 1956. Reprinted in *Administration*, vol. 4, no. 2 and in Basil Chubb and Patrick Lynch (eds.), *Economic Development & Planning* (Dublin, 1969), pp. 48-76. This book is a study of the transition that occurred in the outlook and thinking of Dr Whitaker.
59. Interview of T.K. Whitaker with Bruce Arnold in August 1986.
60. *Ibid*.
61. *Ibid*.
62. Interview of T.K. Whitaker with the author on 2 September 1969.
63. *Ibid*.
64. Source wishes to remain anonymous. Interview with the author.
65. 'Dr. Whitaker Retires', *Public Affairs* (March 1969), p. 4.
66. Interview of T.K. Whitaker with the author on 2 September 1969.
67. Source wishes to remain anonymous. Interview with the author.
68. 'Governor Talks About New Role of Central Bank of Ireland', *Business and Finance* (7 March 1969), p. 12.
69. Interview of Charles Murray with the author, 3 September 1969.
70. Letter dated 19 March 1969 from Dr James Ryan to the author.
71. Interview of T.K. Whitaker with the author of 2 September 1969.
72. Interview of T.K. Whitaker with Bruce Arnold in August 1986.
73. Interview of T.K. Whitaker with Bruce Arnold in August 1986.
74. Letter dated 18 March 1969 from Patrick Lynch to the author.
75. Interview of Jack Lynch with the author on 16 June 1986.
76. 161 Dáil Debates 958, 8 May 1957.
77. Questionnaire received by the author dated 23 January 1969. Respondent wishes to remain anonymous.
78. M. Moynihan, *Speeches and Statements by Éamon de Valera* (Dublin, 1980), p. 466.
79. Interview of Kieran Kennedy with the author on 24 July 1968.
80. Interview of T.K. Whitaker with Bruce Arnold in August 1986.
81. Interview of Éamon de Valera with the author on 3 September 1969.
82. Interview of T.K. Whitaker with Bruce Arnold in August 1986.
83. *Ibid*.
84. Telephone interview of Seán MacEntee with the author on 20 August 1973.
85. Letter to the author from John Healy dated 6 March 1969.
86. *Economic Development*, p. 230.
87. Fanning, p. 516.

88. *Ibid.*
89. *Economic Development*, p. 2.
90. Interview of Kieran Kennedy with the author, 24 July 1968.
91. Interview of T.K. Whitaker with the author, 2 September 1969.
92. Letter dated 19 March 1969 from James Ryan to the author.
93. Interview of Seán Lemass with the author on 14 August 1969.
94. Telephone interview of Seán MacEntee with the author on 20 August 1973.
95. Interview of T.K. Whitaker with Bruce Arnold in August 1986.
96. The *Irish Press*, 25 November 1958, p. 6.
97. The *Irish Times*, 12 November 1958, p. 6.
98. *Economic Development*, inside cover page.
99. The *Irish Press*, 25 November 1958, p. 6.
100. The *Irish Times*, 26 November 1958, p. 6.
101. *Ibid.*
102. *Ibid.*
103. *Ibid.*
104. The *Irish Times*, 12 November 1958, p. 6.
105. *Dáil debates*, 171, 296, 30 October 1958.
106. *Dáil debates*, 171, 432, 3 December 1968.
107. Interview of Seán Lemass with the author, 14 August 1969.
108. *Economic Development*, p. 9.
109. *Ibid.*, p. 218.
110. *Ibid.*, p. 160.
111. *Ibid.*, p. 225.
112. *Programme for Economic Expansion*, p. 22.

T.K. Whitaker on his appointment as Secretary of the Department of Finance (courtesy Irish Press)

Alexis FitzGerald (courtesy G.A. Duncan)

The Genesis of Economic Development

Ronan Fanning

The Whitaker plan proved to be the prelude to the first economic programme, adopted in 1959, the year in which de Valera retired at last from active politics, which he had bestridden like a Colossus for more than four decades. . . . Although it is a dangerous concept to handle, certain stages are best categorized as the supersession of one generation by another. 1880 may very plausibly be represented as such a watershed in Irish history; 1916 as a second. Perhaps we are too close to the event to make a judgement, but all the evidence to hand suggests that 1959 also marked a decisive change in national power and attitude.

> Oliver MacDonagh, *Ireland* (Englewood Cliffs, New Jersey, 1968), p. 132.

The publication of Economic Development *in 1958 suggested that the Government must in future be in a position to appraise national resources, define the principles to be followed and set the targets to be reached in the process of national economic development. The acceptance of this thesis by the Government and the issue of the* First Programme for Economic Expansion *was, perhaps, the most significant event in the history of the Irish civil service in the post-war period.*

> *Report of Public Services Organisation Review Group 1966-69* (*Devlin Report*, Dublin, 1969), 3.1.11.

It was not indeed until a recession in the middle 1950's brought a growing awareness of the gap that was opening up between Ireland and the rest of Europe that a change came. It came with the preparation and publication in 1958 of Economic Development . . . *and the first five-year economic development programme. With dramatic suddenness the state lurched into the middle of the twentieth century, at least so far as the development of the economy was concerned.*

Basil Chubb, *The government and politics of Ireland* (London, 1970), p. 242.

Economic Development . . . *was at once recognised not merely as an important contribution to the economic debate, but as offering a way out of the economic impasse. It is hardly too much to say, indeed, that even today it can be seen as a watershed in the modern economic history of the country.*

F.S.L. Lyons, *Ireland since the Famine* (London, 1971), p. 618.

The dawn that slowly broke over this dismal night was heralded not by some dramatically sudden development nor by some charismatic public figure but by an expert working in the relative obscurity of the civil service. T.K. Whitaker. . . . Never before had the state committed itself to a comprehensive and rational plan for the economy as a whole. It was a new departure also in the more fundamental sense of moving radically away from the old Sinn Féin philosophy of self-sufficiency and industrial protection.

John A. Murphy, *Ireland in the twentieth century* (Dublin, 1975), pp. 142–4.

Although largely ignored by the Press at the time of publication, (Economic Development) *is now generally recognised to have played a key role in redirecting government thinking and in preparing the way for the new economic policies of the 1960s.*

Brendan Walsh, 'Economic growth and development, 1945–70' in J.J. Lee (ed.), *Ireland 1945-70* (Dublin, 1979), pp. 30-1.

The commitment of the Department of Finance to expansionist economic policies was itself revolutionary in the context of Irish governance. Expansionist ideals, insofar as they had existed at all, had hitherto been associated mainly with the Department of Industry and Commerce, which had to fight a regular war of attrition against the Department of Finance. That the premier department should now commit itself to expansion, and expansion through planning at that, marked a historic change in the history of the state.

J.J. Lee, 'Continuity and change in Ireland, 1945–70', in ibid., p. 171.

Most Irish people would still identify 1958–63 as the period when a new kind of Ireland began to come to life. Most associate the successes of those years with a renewed national self-confidence that continues to sustain the country even in its present vicissitudes.

Terence Browne, *Ireland – a social and cultural history 1922-79* (London, 1981), p. 241.

Economic planning may be said to have started in Ireland in 1958, with the publication of the First Programme for Economic Expansion. *This document was a landmark in Irish economic history: for the first time the government set out a comprehensive statement of its policies and objectives, not just for one year ahead but for the following five years. The Programme was also a landmark in that it explicitly admitted that self-sufficiency had failed and it called for a change in policy.*

Peter Neary, 'The failure of economic nationalism' in *Ireland: dependence and independence* (RTE/UCD lectures, *The Crane Bag*, Vol. 8, No. 1, 1984), p. 71.

Where a revisionist new departure was spectacularly evident was in economic organization, for the 1950s saw a resounding rejection of economic nationalism, paradoxically spearheaded by Fianna Fáil. . . . From the mid-1950s it was accepted that traditional nationalist assumptions about the operation of Ireland's economy could no longer be taken as read, since they quite clearly were no longer working.

R.F. Foster, *Modern Ireland 1600-1972* (London, 1988), p. 577.

But enough. Examples abound and further endorsements of the twin truisms underpinning this essay would be redundant.

First, the depth of consensus so early established and so continuously upheld about the way in which *Economic Development* redirected the course of twentieth-century Irish history. For the historians are not alone. Professors of economics, of political science, even of English – to say nothing of civil servants and politicians – all bear similar witness.

Second, the extravagance of language bordering on hyperbole which illuminates this common rush to judgement. MacDonagh's 'decisive change in national power and attitude'; the 'dramatic suddenness' with which Chubb's state lurches into the middle of the twentieth century; Lyons's 'watershed' and Neary's 'landmark' in Irish economic history; Murphy's 'dawn breaking slowly over dismal night'; Walsh's 'key role in redirecting government thinking'; Lee's 'historic change in the history of the state'; Brown's birth of a 'new kind of Ireland'; Foster's 'spectacularly evident' and 'revisionist new departure' – this is language foreign to the austere vernacular of scholarship. That it spreads beyond the confines of disparate disciplines makes it even more remarkable.

By drawing attention to these phenomena, however, I do not seek to dispute the axiom they so powerfully demonstrate: that the publication in 1958 of *Economic Development* and the concomitant Government White Paper, *Programme for Economic Expansion*, were events of truly historic significance. Indeed Brendan Walsh, in a generous review of my own history of the Department of Finance, identified the 'only fault' in 'general approach' as 'a faintly detectable tendency to build [the] story towards a climacteric in the guise of "the emergence of planning" and the 1958 White Paper. The gradual diffusion of some of Keynes's ideas in Ireland is equated a shade too readily with the spread of enlightenment'.[1] Having examined my conscience, I must confess *mea culpa*!

However, that confession only brings us back to our point of departure. And, although it is no part of my purpose to challenge the prevailing orthodoxy about the significance of *Economic Development*, it seems timely to inquire why the consensus about its place as the Great Divide in the history of independent Ireland has been so unanimous and so immoderate.

Part of the answer to that question, like the contours of an iceberg visible above the sea's surface, is plain enough. It is not merely that, as we advance towards the end of the century, 1958/9 more and more neatly bisects all that has happened since 1921, although the attractions of the symetrical must never be entirely disregarded. The substance of the matter is that the first three decades of Irish independence witnessed the ruthless subordination of economic imperatives to the more compelling imperatives of Irish nationalism, and that *Economic Development* brought, and was seen to bring, that era to an end.

'Irish political economy', observed Patrick Lynch in a seminal lecture delivered in 1959, 'unfortunately, sometimes tends to be more political than economic'.[2] He understates the case, at least for the years between the Treaty and the aftermath of World War II. For although that period falls into three distinct phases and although the political factors militating against a dispassionate formulation of the policies best calculated to produce economic development changed somewhat from phase to phase, one overriding factor was common to all three: that from 1922 until 1948 Irish political economy was *always* more political than economic. The Treaty split and the civil war ensured that, after the Union as under the Union, the dynamic of Irish politics drew its energy from the conflict of opinion about the legitimacy of the British connection, albeit in the attenuated form of Dominion status within the Commonwealth accorded to the Irish Free State.

From the outset the struggle for political power hinged on the shape and form of Irish independence, not on the economic policies best suited to a newly independent state. And the transition from the bloody arena of civil war to the more staid and benign forum of the Oireachtas – a change effectively accomplished once Fianna Fáil entered the Dáil in 1927 – left intact that first fact of political life.

It was not just that the collapse of the revolutionary nationalist consensus of 1919-21 focused attention on partisan politics to the detriment of national economics. Civil war also made allies out of former enemies. The beleaguered government of the infant state became beholden to the British government, to the Treasury, to the Bank of England and to the old Anglo-Irish financial community centred on the Bank of Ireland.[3] All thoughts of economic independence, especially associated with the writings of Arthur Griffith and encapsulated in the words 'Sinn Féin', counted for nothing when cast in the balance against the fragile stability of the new state.

The immediate result, in T.K. Daniel's memorable phrase, was to turn 'Griffith on his noble head'.[4] The economic priorities of Merrion Street were founded on the conventional wisdom of Whitehall: budgets must balance; borrowing — especially foreign borrowing — was bad; public expenditure must be pared to the bone, trade must be free; and the Irish currency must remain wedded to the British.

The consequences of this swift and self-imposed denial of the traditional assumptions of Irish economic nationalism proved immense. These assumptions, James Meenan has suggested, were four:

> that the economic development of Ireland was retarded by British misgovernment . . .
> that the economic development of Ireland depends on the policies adopted by the State . . .
> that self-government would almost at once bring economic recovery and prosperity . . .
> that the future of the economy will be determined by what happens in Ireland.[5]

The economic apostasy of the Cumann na nGaedheal government of 1922–32 converted their political opponents to a more fervent economic fundamentalism. Indeed, that a native government's adoption of full-blown policies of economic nationalism was postponed until the first Fianna Fáil government entered office in 1932 arguably deepened both the political and ideological commitment to protectionism. That Fianna Fáil remained in office without interruption until 1948 enhanced this effect and made protectionist barriers more difficult to dismantle than might have been the case had they been erected in the twenties.

The Economic War of 1932–38 is a blatant misnomer. The origins and prolongation of the conflict, for the British as much as for the Irish government, were political; only the weapons were economic. Yet the term serves well to describe the apotheosis of Irish economic nationalism.

Although the collapse of the international free trading system of the twenties and the onset of the global depression which characterised the thirties had prompted protectionist legislation even before the 1932 change of government, the Economic War enabled Éamon de Valera and his cabinet colleagues to weave patriotic virtue out of economic necessity. Once the tariff war had begun, moreover, de Valera denied his officials in the Department of Finance and Department of External Affairs the opportunity to seek an economic solution to what he insisted was a political problem.[6] What was at issue, he told the Fianna Fáil ard-fheis in November 1932, was 'whether the Irish nation is going to be free or not'.[7]

Thus the Treaty had been demolished, the 1937 Constitution enacted and endorsed by popular referendum and de Valera's republic effectively established, before the Fianna Fáil government was willing to enter into the negotiations which ended the Economic War. But those negotiations, culminating in the Anglo-Irish agreements of April 1938, again demonstrated the subordination of economic objectives to nationalistic aspirations. Not until the defence agreement had been negotiated, whereby the British surrendered the ports and all other defence facilities they had retained under the Treaty and so fulfilled the necessary precondition for the free exercise of Irish neutrality in the war already looming with Hitler's Germany, was the way open for the conclusion of the financial and trade agreements. Other more utopian, anti-partitionist aspirations also delayed and, for a time, threatened the success of the negotiations.

Nor did the end of this phase of Anglo-Irish economic conflict pave the way for economic development. Instead a third phase of still greater economic abnormality was inaugurated by the outbreak of World War II. A neutral Ireland with only a tiny, embryonic merchant marine would in any event have been condemned to another, more intensive period of economic stagnation by the isolation imposed by insularity. That the Churchillian response to neutrality included more secret but much more punitive measures of economic warfare,[8] accentuated Irish economic stagnation.

Nor was there any immediate improvement when the war ended. Irish neutrality was not quickly forgotten or forgiven by either the United Kingdom or by the United States — or, indeed, by Canada, the other affluent state which poured economic aid into war-torn Europe. The retrospective economic price of neutrality was high. When it came to supplies of oil, fertilisers and other vital raw materials Ireland languished at the end of the queue.[9]

In sum, then, both domestic and international circumstances conspired against the creation of conditions conducive to economic development during all three phases between 1922 and 1948. The cost of post civil war reconstruction (until 1926-27 the cost of defence and compensation for property losses and personal injuries still ranked among the heaviest charges on public expenditure)[10] was compounded by the cost of what amounted to two successive economic wars. But if the exigencies of political nationalism militated against Irish economic development, so too did certain manifestations of cultural nationalism and of Irish Catholicism.

Although John Hutchinson has recently questioned the assumption that cultural nationalism 'is a "regressive" response to modernization',[11] it is difficult to argue that all the energy and the financial and other resources devoted to the revival of the Irish language and to the nurturing of the Gaeltacht contributed much to the promotion of economic development. Indeed Hutchinson himself acknowledges that, although the Gaeltacht as a

> populist symbol of a simple and dignified Gaelic Ireland, uncontaminated by modern ills, had already been powerfully invoked before 1914 in the words of Hyde and Synge and in the countless polemics of Catholic clerics . . . it had an enhanced power for intellectuals, seeking a national identity appropriate to a small rural democracy and anxious to forget the murderous brutality of a bitter civil war.[12]

Such an anti-materialist ethos was scarcely conducive to economic development. It found its most celebrated expression in the words of Éamon de Valera, most notably in his oft-quoted St Patrick's Day radio broadcast of 1943 when he spoke of 'that Ireland which we dreamed of' as 'the home of a people who valued material wealth only as the basis of right living, of a people who were satisfied with frugal comfort and devoted their leisure to the things of the spirit'.[13]

Such dreams were not the stuff to inspire a drive for economic progress. The inhibiting effect of de Valera's vision on the national psyche was immense and enduring. As late as 1953, for example, during his penultimate term of office as Taoiseach, and in the course of a ringing reaffirmation of the merits of self-sufficiency born of economic nationalism, de Valera invoked Bishop Berkeley's *Queries* which 'just over 200 years ago . . . posed several questions about Ireland's economic development to which we in Fianna Fáil, since we first came into office in 1932, have endeavoured to provide the concrete answers'.[13] It may also be worth remarking that the index to the splendid and meticulous collection of de Valera's speeches and statements where these comments are to be found is innocent of any reference either to T.K. Whitaker or to *Economic Development*, despite the fact that he was still Taoiseach when *Economic Development* was published.

The anti-materialist impulse was not, however, confined to Fianna Fáil. John A. Costello, in a major speech as Taoiseach in 1948, similarly inveighed against 'the dark forces of materialism' while another prominent Fine Gael spokesman, Michael Tierney, wrote of his hopes that World War II 'might be the final stage in the rapid failure of a whole materialistic philosophy of life' leading to the destruction of the 'Anglo-Saxon world order'.[14] Spokesmen for Irish Catholicism were similarly disposed to identify the materialism they so incessantly indicted as Anglo-Saxon.

> Fear of the external modern world was derived in part from a very realistic perception of the frailty of the public ideology which priests and patriotic publicists had constructed. It was felt that it might not survive intact a massive encounter with secular English or American culture. The vulnerability of the ethical system which the priests had built up, and the equally delicate character of the nationalist ideology which the laity had constructed, were well understood.[15]

Throughout the twenties and thirties, at least, the perspectives of

government Ministers and of Catholic bishops were mutually rein-
forcing. This conservative, repressive and authoritarian alliance
between the clerical and political élites offered scant opportunity
for the bureaucratic élite to launch independent initiatives in the
economic arena. That the bureaucracy endured and survived two
traumatic changes of political masters within ten years, in 1922
and in 1932, inculcated an instinct for survival rather than a spirit
of enterprise.

Nor were independent Ireland's academic economists well
placed to launch such initiatives. This was especially true of the
premier colleges in Dublin, closest to the seat of government.
University College's identification with the Cumann na nGaedheal
administration and Trinity's reputation as a Protestant bastion
of Anglo-Irish ascendancy denied credibility to such criticisms
of Fianna Fáil's economic policies as might emanate from their
economists.[16]

In sum, the concatenation of circumstances inhibiting economic
development in Ireland between the Treaty and the end of World
War II was so massive that more than another decade elapsed
before it finally dissolved. Yet, as Roy Foster has observed,
'every historian of twentieth-century Ireland looks for some kind
of anticipation of the 1957-58 démarche into Keynesian expan-
sionism, and locates it somewhere in the 1940s'.[17]

One forcing-house for change was the Commission on Vocational Organisation of 1938-43. Although its episcopal chairman,
Bishop Michael Browne of Galway, was close to Fianna Fáil
Ministers, he proved so trenchant a critic of the bureaucracy that
the Secretary of the Department of Finance, J.J. McElligott,
made a vain attempt to suppress his Commission on the grounds
of war-economy![18] Its report, published in 1944, shows why:
civil servants were painted as timorous, indecisive and procrasti-
nating shirkers of responsibility cowering behind a barrier of
official anonymity.[19] The report, Joe Lee has argued, was 'the
first sustained attempt by a commission since independence to
suggest that normalcy was not enough'.[20]

Two months later another episcopal straw fluttered fitfully in
the wind of change when Bishop Dignan of Clonfert, the then

government-appointed chairman of the National Health Insurance Society, published a pamphlet on social security which attacked the gross inadequacies of the health services. 'That such an influential person as Dr Dignan could condemn existing arrangements as inefficient, degrading and unChristian made wider criticism of the health services legitimate'.[21]

Rumblings of change were also heard in the civil service about the same time. In 1944 Dr James Deeny, a brilliant, energetic and independent-minded Lurgan GP, was drafted as Chief Medical Adviser into the Department of Local Government and Public Health where he wielded the most vigorous of new brooms, notwithstanding early efforts by his new medical colleagues to send him to Coventry.[22] There followed, in December 1946, the creation of two new government departments – Health and Social Welfare. This was the first substantive change in the organisation of central government since the Ministers and Secretaries Act of 1924.

Nor were the mandarins of Merrion Street immune from the contagion of change and T.K. Whitaker has suggested that it was during World War II that officials in the Department of Finance absorbed Keynes's writings and began to relate them to the Irish experience. The Beveridge Report and the British White Paper on Employment Policy gave an added impulse to the process.[23]

The Beveridge proposals also had a catalytic effect on the Irish political élite, especially upon Seán Lemass who initiated a Cabinet Committee on Economic Planning in November 1942. Although this was more a product of short-lived and exaggerated apprehensions about unemployment levels after war ended than a commitment to planning in the sense in which that term was used in the late fifties, and although its procedures were swiftly subsumed into the general work of government, it was another index of changing attitudes.[24]

While there were obvious interactions between these stirrings in the political, bureaucratic and clerical élites, there is no evidence that any one group gave – or sought to give – a clear lead to another. If 'civil servants do not move easily into the camp of change',[25] neither do Irish bishops and politicians.

Seán MacEntee, Minister for Finance in 1932-39 and again in 1951-54, was the most powerful opponent of a change of economic policy inside the Cabinet and he formally drew attention to the conflict between Catholic social teaching and 'Beveridgism'.[26]

The role of Frank Aiken, who looked for and obtained appointment as Minister for Finance when Seán T. O'Kelly was elevated to the Presidency in 1945, was more problematic. Although Aiken, like MacEntee, was never a supporter or admirer of Lemass, he had his own idiosyncratic and, in the eyes of the Finance establishment, unsound views on social credit, cheap money and central banking. But, as Joseph Brennan, then the Governor of the Central Bank, acknowledged, if he could be persuaded to adopt a particular policy 'he had the great advantage that . . . he was able more than any other Minister to secure the agreement of de Valera who had the utmost trust in him'.[27] And this explains why the young Ken Whitaker was first plucked from obscurity in the Department of Finance to serve as personal adviser to Aiken on monetary theory.[28] He was never out of the limelight thereafter.

The general impression of the late forties, then, is more of ferment than of any steady evolution to the climacteric of the late fifties. More ferment was created by the formation, in 1946, of a new republican party with a left-wing social policy. Clann na Poblachta's spectacular by-election successes in October 1947 not only revealed the popular appetite for new directions but precipitated the first change of government for sixteen years.

Both the new Taoiseach, John A. Costello, and the Minister for External Affairs and leader of Clann na Poblachta, Seán MacBride, were given to claiming that their Republic of Ireland Act of 1948 – which finally severed Ireland's last links with the Commonwealth and so swept away all vestiges of ambiguity about Irish sovereignty – had taken the gun out of politics. Given the IRA border-campaign of 1956-62, to say nothing of the much greater recrudescence of political violence since 1969, that claim cannot be sustained.

What can be said, however, is that the 1948 Act took the crutch out of Irish politics: the crutch of that obsession with the

British connection upon which Irish Ministers had leant so long for excuse and explanation when taxed with their indifference to economic development. Why, then, did the gestation of the *First Programme* take another ten years? Perhaps because it was not easy for the disabled — and the ageing disabled at that — to learn to pick their way without crutches across an economic terrain which was unknown to all and which remained alien to many.

Nevertheless, new landmarks were appearing. The Industrial Development Authority (IDA) was established in 1950 and Córas Tráchtála (the Irish Export Board) in 1951. Both were early testaments to what Lemass later described as 'the persistence of doubt about the suitability of Government Departments . . . to operate as development corporations and to perform, in the manner desired, particular functions deemed to be necessary for the nation's progress — functions which require exceptional initiative and innovation'.[29] Yet Lemass had at first been an outspoken opponent of the IDA and was only with difficulty dissuaded from abolishing it when Fianna Fáil returned to power in 1951.[30]

The episode reveals how the ferment of the late forties gave way to a certain floundering in the early fifties. The politicisation of economics had its disadvantages, one of which was Fianna Fáil's initial determination to dispute that any good could come out of the economic initiatives launched by the Inter-Party government of 1948-51. If McGilligan's Dáil speech introducing the first capital budget in 1950 was the earliest 'explicit expression of Keynes in an Irish budget' and a landmark pointing to the shape of things to come, then MacEntee's savagely deflationary budget of 1952 was no less striking a monument to the strength of economic conservatism.[31]

Another notable and somewhat neglected example of how the impact of new thinking was retarded by the partisanship of party politics was the fate of the *Reports of the Commission on Emigration and other Population Problems of 1948-54*. That the Commission was appointed under the warrant of the Minister for Social Welfare and leader of the Labour party, William Norton that its economic advisers were drawn essentially from UCD and Trinity and included John A. Costello's son-in-law (Alexis Fitz-Gerald), that its composition was grossly unrepresentative of Fianna Fáil interests and that its reports were published by the second Inter-Party government a month after it took office in 1954 were reasons enough why they failed to command the kind of consensual support attracted by *Economic Development*. Yet, in retrospect, the language and cast of mind colouring both documents is not dissimilar. This is especially true of the first part of that chapter of the Emigration Commission's majority report relating to population and economic and social development which opens with the assertion that 'much of the evidence submitted to us and many of our discussions were concerned with the extent to which future development of our resources was possible'.

The minority report of Dr Lucey, the Bishop of Cork, also merits this kind of comparative analysis for what it shows of the sustained demand for new directions in the upper echelons of the Catholic Church. And the staccato clarion-call in its final paragraph — 'We have the human resources and we have the material resources for a greatly increased national population. What we lack is the will and the way to use them aright' — might well have found a place in *Economic Development*.

However, although the Emigration Commission's reports did not constitute a programme for immediate action, they further advanced the emergence of that national consensus which proved such fertile ground for the *First Programme*. For in exploring the slowly changing mentalities of the Irish establishment over decades, we must not overlook the factors which finally triggered action in 1957/8. And if a proximate origin not only of *Economic Development* but of its remarkably favourable reception can be identified, it rests somewhere in the national crisis of self-confidence induced by the grotesque haemorrhage of accelerated emigration, revealed by the 1956 census. In this sense 'the preparation of *Economic Development* was, for the participants, *sui generis*, a response to no single major issue but rather to the stagnation that seemed ubiquitous'.[32]

By 1957/8, moreover, the debate on economic development as an imperative of government had been depoliticised as swiftly as economic issues in general had been politicised a decade earlier. One reason for this was electoral politics. The economy had never been the key issue in an Irish election until the Republic of Ireland Act, in Costello's words, had conferred 'complete sovereignty, independence and freedom' and enabled 'the people to centre their energies on the economic problems which had to be met'.[33] The politicians, noted one shrewd observer in 1953, 'have adopted "economics"; they affect an understanding of economic terminology and are courting the affections and interests of professional economists'.[34]

The frequency of general elections dramatically increased the speed of this transition: three times in less than six years, between May 1951 and March 1957, economic issues were flogged to death at the polls. The effect was further enhanced by four changes of government in the nine years between 1948 and 1957. The point was adroitly made by James Ryan, the Minister for Finance who gave the green light to *Economic Development*. Speaking in the Dáil in March 1959, he quoted from four Budget statements made by four successive Ministers for Finance (McGilligan, MacEntee, Sweetman and himself) and defied his audience 'to say who said what. I say that to show that there is really not much between us'.[35]

By 1955, indeed, it might be said that the most significant debates on economic policy were taking place *within*, rather than *between*, the two major parties. The protagonists in the Fianna Fáil debate were Lemass and MacEntee. Lemass seized the initiative when he prepared a memorandum on financial policy for Fianna Fáil's Central Committee in mid-April 1955 which argued for a declaration

> that a future Fianna Fáil government when framing its Budgets will be guided only by consideration of maximum national and social advantage. . . . The tests which a Fianna Fáil government should apply are:
>
> (a) The need to increase the nation's productive power.

(b) The need to achieve full employment and to reduce to a minimum all other forms of waste of economic resources.
(c) The need to raise the living standards of the people and to prevent social injustice.[36]

Although MacEntee's copy of the memorandum is studded with comments and questions — 'What is full employment?' for example — Lemass was not deterred and the upshot was his celebrated '100,000 Jobs Speech' to the party faithful in Clery's Ballroom on 11 October 1955 which was reprinted in a special supplement to the *Irish Press* as his plan for full employment. Jack McCarthy has well described how that speech was quickly absorbed in Fianna Fáil folklore as the moment when Seán Lemass announced Ireland's programme of economic development. He has noted, too, how Lemass armed himself with a copy of Italy's ten-year Vanoni plan while preparing his own *démarche*. [37] Although that episode may seem of small significance, it does reflect a new willingness to look towards broader horizons. These less claustrophobic attitudes, so vital for the creation of an intellectual climate conducive to the ultimate transition from protection to free trade, were given a major boost two months later when Ireland was at last admitted to the United Nations.

Budgetary policy provoked comparable tensions in Fine Gael at the Ministerial meeting in party leader Richard Mulcahy's office in the Department of Education on the evening of 25 January 1957 when Liam Cosgrave, Paddy McGilligan, Tom O'Higgins and John O'Donovan threatened resignation in protest against the proposals of Minister for Finance, Gerard Sweetman, to cut food subsidies in his forthcoming budget. But the split was patched up because the inter-party government were denied the opportunity of framing a budget when Costello dissolved the Dáil rather than face the Clann na Poblachta motion of no confidence tabled by MacBride on 28 January.[38]

Nevertheless, Gerard Sweetman's tenure of office as Minister for Finance did much to pave the way for *Economic Development*. It was Sweetman who, in May 1956, promoted Whitaker to the Secretaryship of Finance in breach of hitherto sacrosanct principles of seniority. And it was Sweetman who established the seminal Capital Investment Advisory Committee and who initiated the Irish application for membership of the International Monetary Fund and of the World Bank – a process which was intimately linked with the immediate origins of *Economic Development*. Indeed, in Whitaker's considered opinion, Sweetman 'was a singularly unfortunate Minister for Finance in as much as his government was overthrown before the "ideas which he implemented" could bear fruit'.[39]

New documentary evidence in files recently released by the Taoiseach's Department sustains the impression of an emerging consensus in 1955-57 on the need for a new departure in economic policy which extended beyond, and owed little to, the confrontations of party politics.[40]

The key figure among the officials in the Taoiseach's Department was Charlie Murray. Nominally a principal officer, Murray's role as economic adviser to the Taoiseach, John A. Costello, was comparable to that played by Patrick Lynch in the first inter-party government of 1948-51.

As the head of a fragile, multi-party coalition encompassing the parliamentary extremes of right and left, Costello experienced continuous difficulty in framing an economic policy which commanded the support of all his cabinet colleagues. His Dáil majority moreover, also depended on the additional support (albeit from outside government) of the Clann na Poblachta party led by Seán MacBride.

Costello and MacBride were both barristers, first drawn together by the freemasonry of the Law Library, and MacBride had a key role in Costello's emergence as Taoiseach in 1948. Their intimacy had flourished around the cabinet table in 1948-51 when MacBride had served as Minister for External Affairs and although he refused a place in the second inter-party government Costello still cultivated his friendship and support.

Costello used Charlie Murray to respond to MacBride's initiatives on economic policy and to temper the harsher policies of his rigorous Minister for Finance, Gerard Sweetman, which posed a permanent threat to the stability of his government.

In July 1956, for example, a fortnight after Seán MacBride had put down a Dáil motion urging the formulation of 'a consecutive and co-ordinated Ten Year Development Plan', Murray initiated inquiries into the functioning of the British Economic Planning Board set up in 1947. Having first established that the Department of Finance knew nothing about the board, he obtained authorisation from Maurice Moynihan, the Secretary to the Government, to ask the Department of External Affairs 'to make discreet enquiries' through the London Embassy.

Although the outcome was that the Board had been ineffective and had 'little more than a "nominal existence" ', that minimal conclusion was deemed sufficiently significant for Murray to cir-culate it on 12 October 1956 to the Taoiseach, to Maurice Moynihan and to his counterpart and namesake, Seán Murray, assistant secretary in the Department of Finance.

A week later Sweetman initiated the Capital Investment Advisory Committee which presented its first report on 22 January 1957.

In the meantime, on 11 January, Costello had given Charlie Murray a copy of MacBride's twenty-six page memorandum of 27 November 1956 on the need for a ten year economic development plan. This was some two months after the Council of Ministers of the Council of Europe had adopted a resolution — (56) 15 — inviting the OEEC to undertake a feasibility study on establishing a fund for the economic development of Southern Europe, and MacBride's memorandum seems to have been a spin-off of his acting as rapporteur to the OEEC on the overall economic position in Europe between July and September 1956.

Although Murray was unpersuaded by the detail of MacBride's arguments, his glosses on the memorandum reveal a measure of agreement at variance with the ferocious opposition MacBride's pronouncements on economic policy in 1948-51 had provoked from J.J. McElligott and T.K. Whitaker in the Department of Finance, and from Joseph Brennan as Governor of the Central Bank.

'Agreed', noted Murray against MacBride's declaration that 'we have never really had any comprehensive economic planning'. He likewise identified MacBride's comment that 'economic activity has to be induced rather than directed' in a free economy as 'the Achilles heel of planning'.

Indeed, as Murray stated unequivocally in introducing his formal response to MacBride's memorandum, there could 'hardly be room for disagreement' with MacBride's basic thesis that all was far from well 'in the body economic. Disagreement in detail with his prescription does not spring from disagreement with his diagnosis'.

Murray noted that

> the need for action, already pressing, is accentuated by the proposal to form a European Free Trade Area. If – as seems likely – the Area is established, the emergence of an integrated West European market of 250 million people will introduce a new and significant element into the present situation which Ireland cannot ignore, whether she joins the Area or not. . . . It is likely that, if we join, our chances of obtaining special arrangements (e.g. in regard to initial exemptions, modifications of the obligation to reduce tariffs etc.,) as a country in process of economic development may be more favourable if we can show that we have a comprehensive and integrated programme for economic development.

Murray's conclusion pointed to 'the possibility of action on the following lines': Ireland's joining the World Bank and asking the Bank to send in a 'general survey mission'; seeking the Bank's assistance to finance investment; sending Irish officials to the Bank's Economic Development Institute – a kind of 'staff college where the participants join in an intensive seminar on the formulation of development policies and the organisation and administration of development programmes; seeking United Nations Technical Assistance; and pressing for the establishmen of Investment and Re-adaptation Funds from which Ireland might hope to benefit in the OEEC discussions about the proposed Free Trade Area.

Although Murray explicitly disavowed any intention of arguing 'the theoretical case for or against planning', his use of quotation drawn from the works of a Professor W.A. Lewis – *The Principle of Economic Planning* (1949) and *Theory of Economic Growth* (1955) – testify to his own conversion to planning. For example

The truth is that we are all planners now. . . . The real choice we have to make is between planning by inducement and planning by direction. . . . The State can plan as much as it wants, but it should plan not by direction but by manipulating the market. . . .

Some planning is necessary, since the results of demand and supply are not socially acceptable in their entirety; but planning can be confined to those spheres where it is considered most important to modify the results that market forces acting alone would yield. . . .

In such matters it is better to rely on figures and hunch rather than upon hunch alone, even when the figures are themselves partly based on hunch.

Murray's memorandum, dated 23 January 1957, was overtaken by the split among Fine Gael Ministers on budgetary policy on 25 January and by the events leading to the fall of the second inter-party government after Clann na Poblachta had withdrawn their support in the Dáil. Nevertheless Costello, who received the memorandum on 28 January, next day directed that a copy be sent to the Minister for Finance, Gerard Sweetman.

Sweetman's speech to the Fine Gael Ard Fheis, on 6 February 1957, uncannily echoed many of Murray's sentiments. Having dismissed long-term economic planning as a chimera of totalitarian states, he appealed for

a sustained and cooperative voluntary effort by our people, with all the aids and inducements democratic institutions can provide, to attain a rising standard of living for a growing population. Whatever targets of national endeavour we may set must be realistic and consistent. Forward thinking about the economic development of the country and what it requires in terms of saving and capital resources generally and how these resources can best be used is essential if our economic and political future is to be secured. . . . What we should do at present is to plan for the years immediately ahead rather than fix our eyes on a horizon we may never reach.

Like Murray, he stressed the implications for Ireland of the EFTA and Common Market proposals. Like Murray, he emphasised 'the need for inducement rather than direction'. Like Murray, he urged close consultation as regards projects and priorities with the Capital Investment Advisory Committee — (which had presented its first report to him on 22 January) – and also with the Agricultural and Industrial Production Councils'.

Although Murray subsequently completed comparable analyses of a trade union pamphlet, *Planning Full Employment*, on 6 February and of Lemass's major speech of 17 January on full employment – copies of which he forwarded to Costello on 7 February and 12 March respectively – the sands of time were fast running out for the government following Fianna Fáil's victory at the polls on 5 March.

The election campaign had thrown the issue of economic planning into still sharper relief. 'The failure of the Government to deal with the economic position' was placed first among the complaints identified in the statement issued by the Ard Chomhairle of Clann na Poblachta on 26 January 1957 to explain their withdrawal of support from Costello's government and which proclaimed that there was 'NO SUBSTITUTE FOR LONG TERM PLANNING'.[41]

MacBride's statement to a meeting of the Clann's Dublin constituency representatives on 30 January focused even more sharply on planning. He rehearsed his continued insistence since January 1956 on 'the urgent necessity to formulate concrete economic proposals' and represented his Dáil motion of 9 July 1956 seeking a ten year development plan as, 'in effect, a vote of censure on the Government' which remained on the order paper of the Dáil. 'Throughout the whole summer', complained MacBride, 'I was told that the Government were preparing an economic programme' and he revealed that he had prepared his extensive memorandum of 27 November 1956 – upon which Charlie Murray had commented in such detail – at Costello's request.[42]

That two members of Fine Gael approached Seán MacEntee and then met de Valera in his room in Leinster House on 5 February to propose an amalgamation of Fianna Fáil and Fine Gael is also indicative of how the economic crisis prompted the emergence of a certain common ground between the two major parties – notwithstanding the fact that Fianna Fáil's Central Committee dismissed the initiative as 'not worthy of serious consideration'.[43]

A larger straw in the wind of change was de Valera's decision not to reappoint Seán MacEntee to the Department of Finance where he had proved so sturdy a pillar of economic conservatism in 1932-39 and in 1951-54. This erosion of the old orthodoxies was marked by the fact, recorded in his diary on 8 March by a disappointed MacEntee, that de Valera 'had already seen Ryan and Aiken before me. He was apparently committed to both'. Ryan got Finance and Aiken External Affairs — the only other 'Ministry' MacEntee wanted.[44]

Charlie Murray availed of the interregnum to produce a seventeen-page commentary, dated 15 March,[45] on the economy under such headings as the balance of payments and external reserves; savings and investment; industrial production and employment; unemployment; the banks and interest rates; and prices and national income. He highlighted 'the problem raised by industrial protection' and pleaded 'for fresh thinking about our protective policy', irrespective about what decisions might be taken about the EFTA proposals.

Murray concluded by pointing to 'the consequences, for employment, emigration and national development, of an inadequate rise in real national income' and referred to Ken Whitaker's seminal paper 'Capital formation, saving and economic progress' delivered to the Statistical and Social Inquiry Society of Ireland on 25 May 1956 — five days before Whitaker was appointed Secretary of the Department of Finance.

The survival of an annotated copy of Murray's memorandum in Ken Whitaker's personal papers indicates that the close co-operation between the two men, which bore fruit in the drafting of *Economic Development*, antedated Fianna Fáil's return to office.

In the meantime, Whitaker, who had gone to Washington to initiate discussions about the prospects of Ireland's joining the World Bank and who returned to Dublin just in time to vote in the general election, had prepared a ten page memorandum entitled 'The Irish Economy, 1957'[46] and dated 21 March 1957 — Jim Ryan's first full day in office as Minister for Finance.

The opening paragraph pulled no punches.

In the *political* field the primary national objective is the re-unification of the country. Until that is achieved, however, and no doubt after it has been achieved, the principal *economic* problem of the Irish Government will continue to be the safeguarding of political independence by ensuring economic viability. Without a sound and progressive economy political independence would be a crumbling façade.

The EFTA proposals, argued Whitaker, by holding a 'mirror up to the Irish economy' had revealed a most disquieting picture. The Department of Industry and Commerce saw no prospect of a large sector of Irish industry surviving 'except with *permanent* protection'; nor did the Department anticipate any significant expansion of Irish industrial exports to 'the Continental part of the Free Trade Area' even if Ireland joined. The Department of Agriculture was equally pessimistic about Irish agricultural exports.

Whitaker saw 'no independent future' for the Irish economy unless competitive Irish export production could be expanded and he hoped that not *'all* industrialists and agriculturalists' shared 'the negative views of the two Departments'. He then came to the heart of the matter.

It is accepted on all sides that we have come to a critical and decisive point in our economic affairs. It is only too clear that the policies we have hitherto followed have not resulted in a viable economy. It is equally clear that we face economic decay and the collapse of our political independence if we elect to shelter permanently behind a protectionist blockade. For this would mean accepting that our costs must permanently be higher than those of other European countries, both in industry and in large sections of agriculture. That would be a policy of despair. . . . The effect of any policy which entailed relatively low living standards here would be to sustain and stimulate the outflow of emigrants and make it impossible to preserve the 26 Counties as an economic entity.

Whitaker argued that 'the challenge of free trade' must therefore be accepted while the 'opportunity for adjustment to freer trading conditions' must be maximised. In a remarkable passage which was tantamount to fluttering a Union Jack under the nose of a Fianna Fáil bull, he suggested that, if we do not expand our production on a competitive basis, we shall have failed to provide the economic basis for the political independence and material progress of the community. Indeed, if we expect to fail, it would be better to make an immediate move towards re-incorporation in the United Kingdom rather than to wait until our economic decadence became even more apparent.

For these reasons the importance of the next five to ten years for the economic and political future of Ireland cannot be over-stressed. Policy must be re-shaped without regard to past views or commitments.

Whitaker proceeded to identify a need 'for harnessing the enthusiasm of the young and buttressing the faith of the active. . . . There is a mood of discontent and despondency abroad, a lack of confidence in the economic future of the country'. He also identified the problems arising from Ireland's close economic association with Britain and, above all, increased agricultural production as 'the most immediate and most important objective of economic policy'. To that end, he recorded, he was already 'engaged (personally as distinct from my Departmental functions) in preparing a memorandum of the facts and considerations which should serve as a guide to agricultural policy' – this was the embryo of the passages on Irish agriculture which formed a major part of *Economic Development*.

Economic policy, Whitaker concluded, should be directed towards five objectives.

The public should be educated to understand that 'better living standards for a larger population 'were dependent on self-help and productive efficiency and on the resources contributed *'out of income* towards capital development'.

Savings, voluntary and compulsory, should be maximised with the objective of financing a development programme 'in which productive projects progressively supersede social investment' and which gave priority to 'the rapid raising of agricultural output'.

The resources available for capital development should be conserved and expanded by curbing the growth of consumption – whether private consumption of less essential goods or public consumption in the form of health and other social services'.

The application of available capital resources should take into

97

account the recommendations of the Agricultural and Industrial Advisory Councils, the Capital Investment Advisory Committee and the World Bank.

Ireland should join the International Monetary Fund and the World Bank and should seek the World Bank's advice 'both technically (through an economic survey mission) and financially (through loans for approved development projects) in the reshaping of our investment programme'.

On 18 April 1957 the Fianna Fáil government duly decided to proceed with the application to join the IMF set in train by Whitaker's visit to Washington in February. The signature of the formal papers in Washington by Irish Ambassador John Hearne was announced in the Dublin papers on 9 August. In mid-September Jim Ryan, Whitaker and J.J. McElligott (the Governor of the Central Bank) represented Ireland for the first time at the annual meeting of the World Bank.

The vehemence and sense of impending doom which so informs this memorandum similarly characterises another eight page memorandum with the apocalyptic title 'Has Ireland a Future?' and excavated from the files recently released by the Taoiseach's Department.[47]

The memorandum, again written in the first person by Ken Whitaker and given by him to Maurice Moynihan in the Taoiseach's Department on 9 December 1957, is clearly an early draft of the introduction to *Economic Development* as published twelve months later. The published version – notwithstanding the status it swiftly and deservedly acquired as a landmark in the history of twentieth-century Ireland – seems strangely bloodless and cautious when compared with the bald, trenchant, ever emotive language of 'Has Ireland a Future?' But this is scarcely surprising in view of the political sensitivity of the issues involved and it remains as a monument to the passions which drove Whitaker, Murray and the other architects of *Economic Development*.

Having explained that the inspiration for the title came from the September 1957 cover of *Dublin Opinion* which depicted Ireland 'as a mature, but still attractive, lady consulting a fortune teller and admonishing her "Get to Work! They're saying I've no future" ', Whitaker spelt out his bleak message:

> Many others besides myself have experienced for some time past a sense of anxiety and urgency about Ireland's economic (and political) future. It would seem that having tried alternative Government [sic] and policies of large-scale capital investment, repatriation of sterling assets, etc., the Irish people are disappointed; and, no longer having anything or anybody but themselves to blame for the continuance of emigration and a relatively slow rate of increase in real income, they are falling into a mood of despondency. After 35 years of native government can it be, they are asking, that economic independence is unattainable and that the political independence achieved with such sacrifice must wither away?

Whitaker went on to deplore the 'vicious circle of increasing emigration, resulting in a smaller domestic market depleted of skill and enterprise', and the 'general air of pessimism' and

> the prospect of the progressive decay of the Irish economy and the undermining of political independence which must accompany it. Even if nationalism be regarded as outmoded in the modern world, it is mere escapism to comfort oneself with thoughts of Ireland's eventual absorption in a bigger and more powerful economy. Patriotism would still require that conditions in the particular local entity known as Ireland should be as agreeable as possible for its people. It seems to me that there is a special obligation on the senior officials of the Irish State to do everything in their power to ensure that the State survives and prospers.

This impassioned appeal to the patriotic instincts of his colleagues in the public service is what most clearly sets 'Has Ireland a Future?' apart from *Economic Development*. But it may be that, by the time of publication, Whitaker felt that his clarion call had been answered. Or it may be that he feared that the severity of his strictures upon the public service might, if published, demoralise as well as inspire.

Noting the administrative legacy bequeathed Ireland by the British, for example, Whitaker suggested that 'we may be more rigid than the British themselves, for instance, in our attitude to the part which public servants may overtly play in helping to form economic policy'. While he accepted that it was essential that civil servants stay out of party politics and maintain their reputation for discretion, he was critical of the fact

> that much of the information which should be the basis of informed public discussion of economic policy tends to be concentrated in Departments and to be made available to the public only in an unco-ordinated way according as it is revealed in Ministerial statements or in Parliamentary discussions.

The British, he suggested, were better at discreetly briefing the press, university economists and other interested parties without incurring imputations of political bias. In a small country like Ireland, he observed astringently,

> where not information only but talent as well is locked up in the Civil Service, it is desirable that there should be freer communication between the service and the public. Even the Border has its 'approved roads'!
> For its undue reticence in the past the Civil Service itself, rather than Ministers, is to blame.

Whitaker went on to acknowledge Ministerial generosity and goodwill from successive governments in permitting and encouraging himself and others 'to undertake work of analysis and research and publish the results'. And he hailed the contribution of the Statistical and Social Inquiry Society of Ireland and the recent advent of the journal *Administration*. But such opportunities were limited and he urged public acceptance that publications such as *Economic Development* 'are objective and not intended to serve the interests of any particular political party'.

The circumstances under which Fianna Fáil resumed power in March 1957 were such as to minimise the possibility that Whitaker's proposals would provoke dissension either within the Cabinet or within the Fianna Fáil party. That Lemass finally succeeded in dissuading de Valera from reappointing the cautious and sceptical MacEntee – and, perhaps, although I have not seen this documented, the idiosyncratic Aiken – as Minister for Finance was crucial. We should remember, too, that although Lemass had by then assumed the mantle of de Valera's heir-apparent, two more years elapsed before he acquired the authority consequent upon appointment as Taoiseach and that the response he still evoked from some of his Cabinet colleagues ranged from the hostility of his rivals for the first place to the suspicion of rural Ministers who distrusted his urbane, metropolitan ways.[48]

Nor should we forget that, though the implementation of the *First Programme* has always been and will remain identified with Lemass, it was de Valera who presided over the public and dramatic reversal of Fianna Fáil's protectionist policies embodied in *Economic Development*. And Brian Farrell's suggestion that 'the continuing presence of de Valera may have provided Lemass with a convenient cloak of seeming changelessness under which new policies, concerns and choices could be exchanged for old'[49] is seductive. Indeed one might go further and question whether such a U-turn could have been so effortlessly accomplished *without* de Valera's endorsement. The benign and emollient yet shrewd and powerful Jim Ryan was, moreover, the ideal Minister for Finance to deflect any residual resentment in the party.

Another point of interest is how far the initiative of officials like Ken Whitaker in Finance and Charlie Murray in the Taoiseach's Department was prompted by a determination not to allow the momentum in the matter of economic planning to rest with the politicians. By 1957/8 Finance officials in particular cannot have been unaware that their Department was only one of an ever-increasing number of players in a more and more frenetic game. The establishment of the Institute for Industrial Research and Standards (1946), of the Shannon Airport customs-free area (1947), of the Organisation for European Economic Development (1948) and of the Council of Europe (1949) — Ireland was a founder member of both organisations, of the IDA (1950), of Córas Tráchtála (1951), of Bord Fáilte and the Irish Management Institute (1952) — to say nothing of the overtures to the World Bank and the IMF and the new-found interest of the Department of External Affairs in economic policy since 1948 — such a proliferation of national and international organisations which would want a finger (or, in some cases, a fist) in the development pie constituted a major challenge to the traditional pre-eminence of Finance in the Irish scheme of things. In this context

Economic Development and, in particular, the breach with the tradition of civil service anonymity which led to its publication under the name of the Secretary of the Department of Finance was a dramatic and effective reassertion of the Department's authority in a changing world. Whitaker's reputation as an economic revolutionary has disguised his achievement as an administrative conservative who not merely preserved the power of the Department of Finance but who established it on a firmer footing than before. The point was hammered home in 1968/9 when Whitaker and Murray convinced the Devlin Review Group into Public Services Organisation that the economic planning function should remain attached to the Department of Finance.[50]

Nor should we overlook the driving power of the Department of Finance's deep-seated tradition of fidelity to British Treasury models. Basil Chubb, whose antennae were always finely tuned to the vibrations of the Irish official mind, neatly anticipated the shape of things to come in a review article entitled 'Treasury Control and Economic Planning' published in the autumn 1956 issue of the influential journal *Administration* which argued that it was

> ... high time that we paid conscious attention to the development of our economic planning and coordinated arrangements. When we do, one thing will surely stand out – if here in Ireland the pattern and temper of Department of Finance control resembles that of the British Treasury, the claim of the Department to the same coordinating role in economic planning will be as strongly based as it will be inevitable.

Finance officials were also conscious of the demands of their political masters that they play a more positive, interventionist role in framing policy and so escape their inverted Micawberesque image caricatured by Whitaker's description of the Finance attitude as waiting for something to turn down.[51] 'Beware of the Department of Finance', Lemass had warned the first Inter-Party government in one of his first Dáil speeches after relinquishing the responsibilities of office for the first time in sixteen years 'it has always been restrictive of development'.[52] And a new Fianna Fáil deputy, delivering his maiden speech in the 1957 budget debate, suggested that

> a tremendous contribution can be made to the solution of our diffi-
> culties by a particular section of the community which has not played
> any great part in this regard up to the present. I refer to our civil ser-
> vants and to the officials of various State bodies. In our civil service,
> we have a reservoir of tremendous talent and ability. As a rule, our
> best people go into the civil service. I feel that, so far, they have in-
> herited a tradition which says they shall aloofly and remotely dispense
> regulations, the purpose of which are no concern of theirs. If we are
> to achieve national recovery, it will involve a tremendous national
> crusade. It must be made clear to our civil servants that they also must
> take part in that crusade. . . .[53]

The crusader was none other than Charles J. Haughey, Seán
Lemass's son-in-law and the personification of Fianna Fáil's
commitment to planning and development in the sixties.

Three days later T.K. Whitaker minuted in the Department
of Finance that it was 'desirable that this Department should do
some independent thinking and not simply wait for Industry and
Commerce or the IDA to produce ideas'; and, at a meeting with
the assistant secretaries, he first enunciated the need 'for some
thinking being done in this Department about the future economic development of the country'.[54] Although the timing may
have been more coincidental than causal and although Haughey's
speech may not necessarily have had Lemass's prior approval,
there can be no doubt that it faithfully reflected the future
Taoiseach's thinking.

Another future Taoiseach, Garret FitzGerald, also highlighted
the significance of the new national consensus in his 1958 com-
posite review of the *First Programme, Economic Development*
and the Capital Investment Advisory Committee's Third Report.

> They have sprung from the crisis of national self-confidence which
> was provoked by the economic difficulties of 1956/7. It seems
> scarcely probable that their authors − whether politicians, civil ser-
> vants, businessmen or economists − would have felt able or, in other
> cases, have been given the opportunity to put forward such radical
> re-appraisals of traditional national policies, had this psychological

crisis not taken place. . . .

The new generation which has grown up in the clamour of constantly reiterated nationalist slogans and catch-cries, was exceptionally unprepared for these events, which superficially at least, seemed to call in question not merely the validity of the policies adopted and applied by successive Irish governments, but even the very economic viability of a separate Irish State. The pent-up but rarely publicly-expressed discontents of this generation which had for years peacefully co-existed with unquestioning acceptance of the nationalist ideal, were suddenly released. . . .

Thus was the ground laid for a re-thinking of national policies along the lines that had hitherto been politically impracticable because of the uninformed state of public opinion.[55]

The Catholic Church, as I have already suggested, also felt the impact of this psychological crisis and changed episcopal attitudes formed part of the new national consensus. Indeed Whitaker cleverly picked his own *imprimatur* in his introduction to *Economic Development* when he cited the words of Dr Philbin, Bishop of Clonfert, in an article published in 1957, as his inspiration.

Our version of history has tended to make us think of freedom as an end in itself and of independent government – like marriage in a fairy story – as the solution of all ills. Freedom is useful in proportion to the use we make of it. We seem to have relaxed our patriotic energies just at the time when there was most need to mobilise them. Although our enterprise in purely spiritual fields has never been greater, we have shown little initiative or organisational ability in agriculture and industry and commerce. There is here the widest and most varied field for the play of the vital force that our religion contains.[56]

Consensus was critical because the larger historical significance of the publication and reception of *Economic Development* was ultimately psychological. Indeed one of its most often quoted passages opens with the assertion that there was 'a sound *psychological* reason for having an integrated development. . . . After thirty-five years of native government people are asking whether we can achieve an acceptable degree of economic progress'. At this level the extraordinary success of *Economic Development* occurred because so many so badly wanted it to succeed. People craved the beat of a different drum and if the tunes to which they now began marching were still patriotic – albeit from a new hymnal of economic patriotism – then so much the better.

Here too, perhaps, lies the explanation of why Ken Whitaker acquired such heroic stature by virtue of *Economic Development* being published over his name. Again, consensus was the key, as we learn from Lemass's fascinating admission to Jack McCarthy that

> publication as an anonymous government publication would give it political aspects which we did not want. . . . The association with the name of a non-political civil servant would help to get its acceptance over political boundaries. . . . It was a deliberate decision, part of our effort to get economic development away from party political tags.[57]

Oliver MacDonagh's point about the historical moments when one generation supersedes another[58] – de Valera getting ready to take his curtain call as Lemass moves centre-stage and Haughey and FitzGerald appear in the wings – is also suggestive. Owen Redmond, Whitaker's immediate predecessor as Secretary of the Department of Finance, first entered the Irish public service in 1906 as a fifteen-year-old clerk in the Office of Public Works,[59] only five years after the death of Queen Victoria and ten years before Whitaker was born. When Whitaker entered the civil service, in 1934, both traumatic changes of government, in 1922 and 1932, were in the past. Redmond had been sixty-two years old when he became Secretary of the Department of Finance. Whitaker was forty. Yet compulsory retirement, even at the age of sixty-five, made it easier to regenerate bureaucrats than politicians. De Valera was seventy-six when, with great reluctance, he finally allowed himself to be persuaded in 1959 to stand down as Taoiseach in the event of his being elected President. And the 'disadvantages and frustrations in being executive officer rather than captain of the ship of state'[60] led Lemass to give vent to an occasional 'tirade' against his ageing Chief.[61]

Lemass's own terse, pragmatic and consciously anti-charismatic style of leadership further contributed to the circumstances in which Whitaker found himself cast in a starring role. The heroes of Ireland's new generations were apolitical. It seemed appropriate, for example, that it was Whitaker who succeeded de Valera as Chancellor of the National University of Ireland in 1976, and unsurprising that his name should figure prominently in speculation about non-party candidates for the Presidency in the mid-seventies.

That so much national hope and expectation was invested in *Economic Development* was a dimension of the problem it sought to redress and of its success in epitomising a new national mood. That economists writing since the seventies have 'tended to the view that the whole planning exercise was seriously flawed from a methodological point of view'[62] is beside the point.

John Bradley's reminder that, 'by the standards of the late 1970s and the 1980s, the decade following *Economic Development* was truly a golden age of sustained high growth and low unemployment'[63] also helps to explain how it so soon acquired a heroic perspective. For, as Ken Whitaker himself has recently written, 'the withering of the bloom from the end of the decade onwards has enhanced rather than dimmed the bright memory of the 1960s'. That those years 'have in retrospect, taken on the aspect of a Paradise Lost' and that our membership of the European Economic Community since 1973 cannot 'be headlined as Paradise Regained'[64] is not the fault of those who first nurtured the bloom.

NOTES

1. Brendan Walsh's review of Ronan Fanning, *The Irish Department of Finance 1922–58* (Dublin, 1978) – hereafter cited as Fanning, *Finance* – in *Irish Economic and Social History*, vii, (1980), p. 122.
2. Patrick Lynch, 'The economics of independence: some unsettled questions of Irish economics' in Basil Chubb and Patrick Lynch, *Economic Development and Planning* (Dublin, 1969), p. 129.
3. This theme is elaborated in Ronan Fanning, 'The impact of independence' in F.S.L. Lyons (ed.), *Bicentenary Essays – Bank of Ireland 1783–1983* (Dublin, 1983), pp. 65–77; see also Fanning, *Finance*, chapts. 2–4.

4. T.K. Daniel, 'Griffith on his noble head: the determinants of Cumann na nGaedheal's economic policy, 1922–32' in *Irish Economic and Social History*, iii, (1976), pp. 55-65.

5. James Meenan, *The Irish Economy since 1922* (Liverpool, 1970), pp. 270-4.

6. Cf. Fanning, *Finance*, chpt. 7.

7. Maurice Moynihan (ed.), *Speeches and Statements by Eamon de Valera 1917-73* (Dublin, 1980), p. 277.

8. See Robert Fisk, *In Time of War – Ireland, Ulster and the Price of Neutrality 1939-45* (London, 1983), pp. 252-72.

9. Cf. Ronan Fanning, *Independent Ireland* (Dublin, 1983), pp. 153-4.

10. *Ibid.*, p. 39.

11. John Hutchinson, *The Dynamics of Cultural Nationalism – The Gaelic Revival and the Creation of the Irish National State* (London, 1987), p. 9. It is noteworthy that Hutchinson's book devotes scant attention to economic policy.

12. *Ibid.*, p. 318.

13. Moynihan, *De Valera*, p. 565.

14. See Ronan Fanning, *"The Four-Leaved Shamrock": Electoral Politics and the National Imagination in Independent Ireland* (Dublin, 1983), pp. 16-17.

15. Tom Garvin, 'Priests and Patriots: Irish Separatism and Fear of the Modern, 1890-1914', in *Irish Historical Studies*, vol. xxv, no. 97 (May 1986), p. 80.

16. Cf. Ronan Fanning, 'Economists and Governments: Ireland 1922-52' in Antoin E. Murphy (ed.), *Economists and the Irish Economy* (Dublin, 1983), pp. 138-56.

17. Foster, *loc. cit.*

18. Cf. Fanning, *Finance*, pp. 322-3.

19. Cf. Fanning, *Independent Ireland*, p. 158.

20. Joseph Lee, 'Aspects of corporatist thought in Ireland: the Commission on Vocational Organisation, 1939-43' in Art Cosgrove and Dónal McCartney (eds.), *Studies in Irish History presented to R. Dudley Edwards* (Dublin, 1979), p. 344.

21. Ruth Barrington, *Health, Medicine and Politics in Ireland 1900-70* (Dublin, 1987), p. 152.

22. See James Deeny, *To Cure and to Care – Memoirs of a Chief Medical Officer* (Dublin, 1989).

23. See Fanning, *Finance*, pp. 357, 384-6.

24. *Ibid.*, pp. 352-3 and *Independent Ireland*, pp. 150-3; but cf. Brian Farrell, *Seán Lemass* (Dublin, 1983), pp. 65-9.

25. Chubb and Lynch, *op. cit.*, p. 362.

26. See Farrell, *loc. cit.*

27. Leon Ó Broin, *No Man's Man – A Biographical Memoir of Joseph*

Brennan (Dublin, 1982), p. 153.
28. See Fanning, *Finance*, pp. 392–3.
29. See Seán Lemass, 'The Organisation behind the Economic Programme', an address delivered on 22 April 1961 and published in Chubb and Lynch, *op. cit.*, pp. 206–7.
30. See Farrell, *op. cit.*, pp. 82–3 and Ronan Fanning, 'Alexis FitzGerald' in Patrick Lynch and James Meenan (eds.), *Essays in Memory of Alexis FitzGerald* (Dublin, 1987), p. 8.
31. Cf. Fanning, *Finance*, pp. 456–60, 482–4.
32. *Ibid.*, pp. 515–16.
33. *Irish Times*, 15 Nov. 1948.
34. Desmond Williams, writing in *The Statist* of 24 Oct. 1953.
35. *Dáil debates*, 173, 1078; cf. Lynch, 'Economics of Independence', p. 128.
36. MacEntee papers, P 67/53/1, Archives Dept., University College Dublin.
37. See above, p. 26.
38. See above, p. 34.
39. Fanning, *Finance*, pp. 503–11.
40. All otherwise unattributed references in what immediately follows are drawn from SPO S 16066A (National Archives).
41. MacEntee papers, P67/390 (3).
42. *Ibid.*, P67/390 (4).
43. The *Irish Press*, 11 Feb. 1957.
44. MacEntee papers, P67/815 (4).
45. I am most grateful to Dr T.K. Whitaker for lending me this memorandum.
46. *Ibid.*
47. SPO S 16066A (National Archives).
48. See Fanning, *Independent Ireland*, pp. 147–8.
49. Farrell, *Lemass*, p. 96.
50. See Fanning, *Finance*, pp. 623–5.
51. *Ibid.*, p. 564 *et seq*.
52. *Dáil debates*, 110, 253; 9 March 1948.
53. See Martin Mansergh (ed.), *The Spirit of the Nation – the Speeches of Charles J. Haughey* (Cork & Dublin, 1986), p. 2; 14 May 1957.
54. See Fanning, *Finance*, p. 509.
55. Chubb and Lynch, *op. cit.*
56. *Economic Development*, paragraph 21 – the passage is taken from an article published in the autumn 1957 number of *Studies*.
57. See above, p. 57.
58. See above, p. 74.
59. See Fanning, *Finance*, pp. 492–3.
60. Brian Farrell, *Chairman or Chief – The Role of the Taoiseach in Irish*

Government (Dublin, 1971), p. 57.

61. Margaret MacEntee was the recipient of one such outburst – see Mac-
    Entee's gloss on Farrell, *loc. cit.*, MacEntee Papers, P 67/33/2.
62. Walsh, 'Economic Growth and Development', pp. 35–6; see also Kieran
    A. Kennedy, Thomas Giblin and Deirdre McHugh, *The Economic
    Development of Ireland in the Twentieth Century* (London, 1988),
    pp. 66–7.
63. See below, p. 138.
64. 'Ireland's Development Experience', a paper read to the Annual Con-
    ference of the International Development Studies Association in Dublin
    on 24 Sept. 1982 and published in T.K. Whitaker, *Interests* (Dublin,
    1983), p. 1.

James Ryan (courtesy G.A. Duncan)

Charles Murray (courtesy G.A. Duncan)

Economic Development in Historical Perspective

J.J. Lee

Planning was something of a dirty word in many quarters in post-war Ireland.[1] This was axiomatically the case for exponents of *laissez-faire*, like J.J. McElligott, the powerful Secretary of the Department of Finance, 1927–53, and his close friend, Joseph Brennan, Governor of the Central Bank, 1943–53. They held tenaciously to the view that virtually all government intervention was bound to be detrimental to economic development. The prime function of government, in their view, was to spend as little as possible, hold taxation as low as possible and rely on the un-impeded functioning of the market to ensure maximum profits for farmers and businessmen, who would in turn respond to the profit incentive by increasing production and thus creating employment. Brennan and McElligott were not isolated exceptions. Not only did they command powerful positions, but they could also be confident of support from most officials in the Department of Finance, from the banking community, and from leading members of the small fraternity of economists in the country at the time, including the holders of the two chairs of Economics in Dublin, George O'Brien at University College and George Duncan at Trinity. O'Brien was rather less dogmatic than Duncan, but continued to hold steadfastly to the principles he attributed to Patrick Hogan, Minister for Agriculture 1922–32, in his classic obituary of Hogan, who was killed tragically in a car crash in 1936.

> Hogan started from the assumption that agriculture was, and would remain, by far the most important industry in the Free State, and that the touchstone by which every economic measure must be judged was

112

its effect on the prosperity of the farmers. He believed that economic policy should be directed to maximise farmers' income, because, the farmers being the most important section of the population, everything that raised their income raised the national income of the country.

Prosperity among farmers would provide the purchasing power necessary to sustain demand for non-agricultural goods and services, and it was useless to encourage secondary industries unless the primary industry was in a position to purchase their products. The principle aim of agricultural policy in the Free State should therefore be the maximisation of the farmers' income. . . . Here, therefore, were the data of the problem with which Hogan was confronted. 1. agricultural policy must be directed towards the maximisation of the farmers' profit; 2. the farmers' profit is the difference between what they put into the land and what they take out of it, i.e. the difference between costs of production and selling prices; 3. selling prices were, in most cases, outside the control of the Free State government. When the problem was stated in this way it becomes obvious that the only thing the government could do to help the farmer was to assist him to reduce his costs of production.[2]

Although Hogan himself was not ideologically committed to *laissez-faire*, this serves as an effective exposition of the assumptions underlying the philosophy of the Department of Finance, the Central Bank and the dominant economists in the post-war period. It reposed its faith, it will be clear, in creating a 'climate' conducive to investment, from which growth would follow.

Despite the distinction of its exponents and the vigour of its exposition, this view had not commanded the high ground of policy-making during the thirties. Once Fianna Fáil came to power in 1932, committed to an industrialisation policy based largely on protectionism, and to self-sufficiency rather than international competitiveness in agriculture, the votaries of *laissez-faire* found themselves rapidly on the defensive. The Department of Finance had to cede ground to the much more interventionist Department of Industry and Commerce, whose Secretary, John Leydon, a former Finance man, or 'game keeper turned poacher', as McElligott sourly observed, ably assisted his dynamic new minister, Seán Lemass, in implementing a vigorous policy of intervention.[3] When Per Jacobsson, the eminent Swedish economist, served on the Banking Commission, chaired by Joseph Brennan, in the period 1934-38, he found 'planning' to be a quite fashionable concept in Irish government, caustic though he was about Irish ability to plan.[4] During the War, the Cabinet established a committee on economic planning, consisting of the Taoiseach himself, Éamon de Valera, Lemass as Minister for both Supplies and Industry and Commerce, and the Minister for Finance, Seán T. O'Kelly. The Committee met more than fifty times between 1942 and 1945.[5] Indeed, Lemass contemplated a permanent super-ministry which he envisaged as a virtual central planning agency with extensive powers of intervention and direction in the economy, far exceeding anything attempted subsequently.[6]

Although the Lemass penchant for *dirigisme* may not have been widely shared, there was a much greater receptivity to the general idea of planning than would be the case in the post-war decade. The Commission on Vocational Organisation, which sat from 1939 until 1943 under the chairmanship of Dr Michael Browne, Bishop of Galway, and included representatives of a wide range of social and economic interests, sharply criticised the State for its failure to plan properly. The *Report* of the Commission was, it is true, highly critical of the civil service. But this was not because of its interventionist propensities but because of the inefficiency of its intervention. It recommended, not the abolition of 'planning', but rather the transfer of planning functions from the civil service — which it held to be too rigid and unimaginative in its thinking — to a National Vocational Council, representative of a wide range of interests in the country, which it felt would plan more imaginatively and effectively. Irrespective of the feasibility of the Commission's proposals, it is clear that it wanted a much more vigorous sense of 'planned' national development.[7] One might have felt, therefore, that the country was poised for a leap — whether forwards or backwards is a matter of taste — into 'planning' once the end of the War allowed policy-makers to think in more expansive terms once more. Instead, planning lost caste, and to such an extent that Mr Whitaker took some pains to emphasise that *Economic Development* was *not a* plan, but merely a programme.

There are a number of explanations for the devaluation of the semantic coinage of planning after the War. Firstly, the potential planners fell out among themselves. Lemass responded furiously to what he felt to be unjustified criticisms of 'his' Department of Industry and Commerce in the *Report of the Commission on Vocational Organisation*, which he dismissed brusquely as a 'slovenly' document.[8] The issue of planning itself tended to be lost sight of in wrangling over who should 'plan'. As it became clear that the idea of vocational planning was rejected by government and by virtually all main departments, whatever their internal differences, the wide but diffuse body of opinion sympathetic to vocationalism, including many churchmen, came to prefer no planning to State planning. This instinct was reinforced by the anti-communism that grew more widespread as the Cold War intensified, and as communism came to be identified with anti-Christ in Irish popular imagination. As communism was also identified with Stalin's five-year plans, planning could be denounced as not merely subversive of the economic law of the market, but of the divine law as well. A *mélange* of motives and instincts thus coalesced to enable anti-planners to capture the high ground of public instinct in these matters.

Lemass continued to support planning, or at least vigorous intervention. Indeed, his initial proposals for an Industrial Efficiency Bill in 1946 went beyond even his thinking of the Second World War on the need for vigorous government intervention, even to the extent of planning individual private enterprises, and if necessary nationalising them.[9] But his position within government weakened, and the Cabinet frustrated most of his interventionist proposals between 1945 and Fianna Fáil's loss of office in early 1948. The post-war government, too, was in general a tired government, largely drifting and, until the sudden emergence of Clann na Poblachta whose threat did not fully crystalise until its spectacular by-election victories in October 1947, complacent in the conviction that 'there was no alternative' and that it could enjoy office indefinitely without doing anything in particular.

It was a matter of particular irony that the initial post-war impetus towards planning should have come not from the Russians, but from the Americans. The Truman administration made it a pre-condition of Marshall Aid that supplicant countries should submit a national economic plan providing some indication of how the money would be used, and the results expected. The Irish effort in this direction, ambitiously entitled *Long-term recovery programme*, was completed in October 1948 and published in January 1949. The programme provides a useful pointer to the capacity of politicians and civil servants to plan at that stage. It is not uncharitable to say that it bears no relation to a programme, much less a plan. It was a jumble of statements thrown together in order to extract as much as possible from the Americans. It made no effort at realistic projections. The programme was cobbled together by a handful of officials, including Freddy Boland at the Department of External Affairs and Tom Murray at the Department of Industry and Commerce.[10]

There would have been no programme at all, simply because there would have been no application for Marshall Aid, if the Department of Finance had had its way. But Finance had been outmanoeuvred by the Department of External Affairs even before Seán MacBride became Minister for External Affairs in the first inter-party government that took office in March 1948. MacBride was crucial in the formation of the coalition government, and exerted immense influence on general policy, at least in the early months of the new régime. One of the first decisions taken by the new government was that the Department of External Affairs would be responsible for the Marshall Aid Programme. This circumvented the opposition of Finance, suspicious that the money would be squandered on corrupt, or at least futile, political investment projects. There was indeed always that danger. The danger was all the greater in that Finance, steeped in negative thinking, had no positive proposals of its own. It was, therefore, inevitable that proposals from other departments would expand to fill the vacuum. It was not, of course, the function of Treasuries in other countries to suggest expenditure either. It was their classic function to control and limit it. But Ireland was so barren of ideas for productive expenditure and was at such a particular stage of development, that it was unfortunate that some of the best natural minds in the country should have become so habituated to thinking in purely blocking terms. In any case, the *Long-term programme* exposed the unpreparedness of the official mind at that stage, when confronted with the challenge of devising a development programme for Ireland.

It is true that many of the programmes submitted by other applicants for Marshall Aid also relied heavily on imagination. But even understanding colleagues in the OEEC, who were obliged to offer some commentary on the Irish submission, requested further information on investment policy 'about which we have given little information', and also about 'internal consumption levels: the memo did not say much on this matter. . . .'[11] These may appear innocent requests. But the reader is instantly alerted by reference to 'investment' and 'consumption'. These were after all the key variables in the Keynesian revolution, whose implications for an interventionist policy McElligott and his cohorts at Finance were doughtily resisting.

It is not our concern here to ponder the validity of Keynesian theory or to assess the interminable debate it has provoked among economists. Suffice it to say that had Keynes never existed, coherent economic planning could not have proceeded without adequate information on investment and consumption. They were key variables in the economic régime, irrespective of the policies which might be formulated in relation to them. Finance had succeeded in largely ignoring them, and even failed to collect information about them, because of its assumption that as the market reigned supreme, it did not matter what their levels were. The levels would always be right in the best of all possible worlds if only government refrained from interfering with the market mechanism. The failure of the *Long-term programme* to 'say much' on these matters reflected primarily the simple absence of adequate information at the disposal of the official mind about these matters. It is also true that public servants viewed the *Long-term programme* mainly as 'an exercise that had to be undertaken to persuade the Americans to give us Marshall Aid'.[12] It should not, therefore, be regarded as an infallible indicator of what they could have done, had they chosen to do it seriously. But the will was still lacking at this stage.

Finance continued as resolutely opposed to government attempts to activate the economy after the *Long-term programme* as before. When it was proposed in 1948 to establish an Industrial Development Authority, whose main function should be 'to initiate proposals and schemes for the creation and development of Irish industry', Finance reacted with scorn. It did not want the Authority created at all, but if the worst came to the worst then its function should be to supplement private enterprise, not to supplant it. It should have no independent power to take steps without government approval. Finance did not mince its reasons. Proposals should go to Cabinet 'insofar as Cabinet is protection against foolish or corrupt ministers'.[13] Rarely has the mandarin disdain for either the competence or the integrity of the products of the democratic process in Ireland been so crisply articulated. The IDA should be constituted in a manner that would win the confidence of the business community who 'must feel from the start that they will get a fair crack of the whip and that the Board is not a gang of crack-pot socialist planners'.[14] The doctrinaire basis of the Finance mind could scarcely be expressed more emphatically.

> The Board, [Finance insisted] should not be envisaged as a Board of mastermind planners — to direct and plan the industrial development of the country, but rather as a Board of factfinders and advisors to the community and the government on the activities of private enterprise. They are there to search out possibilities of industrial development, to collect facts and statistics and to bring them to the notice of entrepreneurs in some fair and suitable manner. It should definitely *not* be within their scope or function to themselves . . . plan industry or any branch thereof. They should be purely an industrial development advisory board and it might be as well to title them as such.[15]

Even this statement, uncompromising though it may appear represented a retreat from the standard Finance position. Thi was based on the axiomatic assumption that private enterprise was so enterprising there was no possibility that it could be overlooking, thanks to the clock-like functioning of the market mechanism, any possible opening for profit. The admission that there might be some possibilities that entrepreneurs had overlooked was actually a major concession, however slow the Department would be to draw the implications for itself. It continued to view 'planning', under which it included any suspicion of Keynesianism, with its implication that government could significantly influence the level of economic activity, with intense suspicion. Indeed, one of the more bizarre submissions made to an Irish Cabinet came from Finance in 1953, when it snatched at some comments in the *Financial Times*, and at an article in the *Neue Zürcher Zeitung*, to suggest that Ireland was suffering from the same *over*-employment syndrome as Sweden – a Sweden which had hitherto been held up as a cynosure of the success of planning, and which was now poised, in Finance's hopeful scenario, to plunge into depression.[16] Sweden did not plunge into depression, and the majority of the Irish found difficulty in persuading themselves that they were suffering from over-employment, at a time of an official 9 per cent unemployment rate, vastly augmented by the massive under-employment in agriculture, reflected in rising emigration levels, whose rate had not been exceeded since the 1880s. One could not have predicted, on the basis of the intellectual performance of Finance in the early fifties, that before the end of the decade it would prove capable of producing as impressive a document as *Economic Development*. What happened?

The dramatic shift that occurred in a five year period – the first real shift in the ethos of Finance since the foundation of the State – owes its origins to a combination of factors involving fundamental changes of personalities, and of objective economic and political circumstances.

Joseph Brennan resigned as Governor of the Central Bank in 1953 after a period of poor relations with the government. It would be reassuring to think that this was the result of a reasoned intellectual disagreement between himself and the Minister for

Finance, Seán MacEntee. It was not. MacEntee largely subscribed to Brennan's deflationary and *laissez-faire* instincts. But Brennan had taken to expressing these with a degree of disdain for government policy-makers that they no longer felt able to tolerate.[17] The knock-on effects were more significant. To take Brennan's place, McElligott was shifted from Finance, creating a vacancy in the most important of all administrative posts for the first time in twenty-six years. It would be reassuring to think that this was done with a view to initiating fundamental reassessment of economic policy. It was no such thing. It was essentially to pre-empt a potentially embarrassing public debate for the government. The Cabinet had no particular views about replacing McElligott with a different type of official. It therefore took the obvious option of promoting the next in line, the sixty-two-year-old Owen Redmond, who had entered as a junior clerk in 1912 and worked his way up.[18] Redmond had only three years to serve and it would have been unreasonable to expect fresh initiatives in the circumstances.

The Department of Industry and Commerce had traditionally served as the main innovating Department in government, with Finance as the main blocking Department. But the role of Industry and Commerce had declined since 1948, when Fianna Fáil lost office and Lemass went into opposition after sixteen years as minister. His successor, Daniel Morrissey, did not convey the same sense of energy. Lemass, it is true, returned to office in 1951 and took a number of initiatives. But he was himself fighting ill health and had to take second place to MacEntee and Finance in the formulation of economic policy. He went into opposition once more when Fianna Fáil lost office in 1954. His successor as Minister, William Norton, though leader of the Labour Party and an accomplished grassroots politician, was not of comparable stature. John Leydon, the powerful Secretary of Industry and Commerce since 1932, probably felt his job satisfaction declining following the departure of Lemass. It is doubtful if he felt the same respect for Morrissey or Norton. He took the opportunity to resign at the age of sixty in 1955. The Industry and Commerce of the mid-fifties was no longer the dynamo of twenty years before, or even ten years before, and it was unlikely that fresh ideas would now emerge from that quarter.

The traditional innovatory role of Industry and Commerce had been partly taken over by the Department of External Affairs in 1948-51. Seán MacBride took a keen interest in economic development, which his crucial political role in the government allowed him to indulge to a much greater extent than had hitherto been customary in a Cabinet tradition where ministers were largely expected to mind their own departmental business. But External Affairs' role also contracted after 1951. MacBride lost office, never to resume it. Perhaps equally importantly, the Secretary of External Affairs, F.H. Boland, who had once worked in Industry and Commerce, and had one of the most sagacious minds in the public service, went to London as Ambassador in 1950. Nor were initiatives likely from other departments. In what seems a panic meeting of the Secretaries of the main economic departments and the Department of the Taoiseach in January 1957, both Industry and Commerce, and Agriculture appear as virtually burned out volcanoes, clinging to recipes that had failed to deliver the goods and the jobs in recent years, whatever degree of success they may have achieved in earlier decades.[19] The prospects for the economy and the country looked decidedly bleak, insofar as they depended on innovatory thinking from the heads of government departments. No-one at that stage, it is probably true to say, thought of looking to Finance for 'a great deed'. Who could have blamed them, in the light of the Department's track record? Yet it was from this unexpected quarter that the initiative would come that would help foster the dramatic change of mood that would launch the country onto a new trajectory in a few years.

The alarm felt in official circles at the economic crisis of the mid-fifties was graphically reflected in the appointment of T.K. Whitaker as Secretary of Finance in 1956. In contrast to the situation three years before, when Owen Redmond had succeeded McElligott as next in line, the Minister for Finance, Gerard Sweetman, now 'passed over' the next in line, to nominate the forty-year-old Whitaker. Whitaker was indeed pre-eminent in terms of ability, but that was no guarantee that he would be appointed. The personal difficulties that could arise in small departments – and all Irish departments were small – as well as deep-seated instincts in Irish administrative culture, gave the inside track to the senior contender. Only a consciousness of exceptional crisis normally sufficed to overcome the inhibitions inherent in the culture. Whitaker would quickly vindicate his appointment – indeed, it is not inconceivable that his feeling that he *must* vindicate his appointment may have spurred him to finding a way of making an immediate and emphatic mark. It is by no means clear, however, that it was the intention of Gerard Sweetman, a vigorous but traditional conservative, that Whitaker should come to be remembered as an expansionist, even if a cautious one, rather than as a supreme exponent of 'not an inch'. In Sweetman's scenario, it was as likely that Whitaker would come to fulfil the McElligott law as to destroy it. This must remain speculative, but Sweetman proved an ardent advocate of retrenchment as Minister, and showed scant sympathy for more adventurous approaches to economic policy. Whitaker too had distinguished himself hitherto less as a radical innovator than as an exceptionally effective advocate of the conventional Finance wisdom. But circumstances and personalities were once again conspiring to propel him in a fresh direction.

The Cold War began to thaw somewhat with the death of Stalin in 1953, even if East-West relations remained strained. 'Planning' came to be disengaged, at least in some minds, from the Russian experience, as news began to filter through about the Monnet plans in France and the Vanoni plan in Italy. The insularity of Irish thinking may have meant that only a small proportion of policy-makers heard of these, much less wrestled with their implications. But at least advocates of planning could now point out that there were non-Communist versions which had not brought to chaos the Western societies that embraced them. At home too, whatever the dangers of planning might be, the crisis that seemed to have descended from the early fifties and to have accentuated in the mid-fifties with further harsh supplementary budgets in 1956, impressed on a number of intelligences that existing policies simply had to be revised, whatever the alternatives might be.

Indications of a more receptive attitude could be detected when Patrick Lynch published a seminal article on 'Economists and Public Policy' in *Studies* in 1953. Lynch was a young Economics lecturer in UCD, who had joined the Department of Finance after graduation and then moved to the Department of the Taoiseach where he exerted considerable influence on the economic thinking of John A. Costello, and of Patrick McGilligan, Minister for Finance, 1948–51. Lynch was one of the earliest advocates of Keynesianism amongst Irish economists. Widely read, bringing both an historical and a comparative perspective to bear on economic development, he subjected the traditional assumptions of Finance to critical scrutiny. In his 1953 article, he distanced 'planning' from the Communist versions and made an intellectual case that proved difficult to refute. He did so with the sensitivity of the insider to realities of decision making, and his ideas infiltrated the intellectual infra-structure in the mid-fifites. Whitaker had initially responded unenthusiastically to the suggestion that Finance should try to take the public into its confidence and restore faith in the quality of the official mind by issuing a series of White Papers whose self-evident intellectual power would compel public admiration. To Whitaker, the real quality of the official mind was to be displayed in memoranda and marginalia, not in publications.[20] But the crisis of intellectual confidence which followed from the economic crisis in the mid-fifties persuaded Whitaker of the merit of Lynch's view.

In addition to the intellectual issues involved, neither institutional nor party politics should ever be overlooked in an Irish, any more than in any other, decision-making context. Both probably played some part in impelling Whitaker in the direction of *Economic Development*.

Whitaker was the youngest Secretary of any Department in 1956. He himself needed a distinctive achievement to assert his pre-eminence. Finance, although still the predominant Department of State, might not always remain so. In particular, it might feel under threat once Fianna Fáil returned to government in March 1957. This was not because of any inherent hostility of de Valera to Finance. But de Valera seemed likely to retire shortly. His successor was widely expected to be Seán Lemass. Lemass and Finance had engaged in many a herculean struggle in the previous twenty-five years. Lemass had now finally established his ascendancy in the party over Seán MacEntee, closest to the Finance heart as a defender of conservative economic values. It was by no means certain that Lemass, still restless for an expansionist thrust, as revealed most starkly in his Clery's speech in 1955 – reprinted for electoral purposes during the 1957 campaign – might not attempt a dash for growth by thrusting Finance aside and either favouring 'his' Department of Industry and Commerce or establishing a super-department, as he had earlier advocated. In any case, Lemass must have appeared dangerously unpredictable from a Finance perspective. Given the obvious dearth of initiative in other departments, what more effective way to consolidate the dominance of Finance, than to devote 'some thinking' to 'the future economic development of the country' as Whitaker urged on his senior officials in May 1957?[21] In the event, *Economic Development* would admirably suit Lemass's political and policy needs.

Although the *First programme for economic expansion*, the White Paper based on *Economic Development*, was rather more industry oriented than *Economic Development* itself, which continued to repose considerable confidence in Patrick Hogan's recipe, Lemass was only too happy to present the White Paper as the incarnation of the 'non-political' expert wisdom of the Department of Finance – ironically for one who had spent so much of his life locked in close combat with Finance. While this suited Lemass, it also suited Finance. Whitaker, at a stroke, established his own primacy as the outstanding civil servant of his day, reinforced the primacy of his Department, and made a major contribution to the welfare of his country.

NOTES

1. This essay draws substantially on sections of my *Ireland 1912-1985: Politics and Society* (Cambridge, 1989), and on the sources there cited.
2. George O'Brien, 'Patrick Hogan', *Studies*, 25 (September 1936), p. 358.
3. Ronan Fanning, *The Irish Department of Finance 1922-58* (Dublin, 1978), p. 258.
4. Ronan Fanning, 'Economists and Governments: Ireland 1922-52', in A. Murphy (ed.), *Economists and the Irish Economy* (Dublin, 1984), p. 150.
5. Joseph Lee and Gearóid Ó Tuathaigh, *The Age of de Valera* (Dublin, 1982), p. 159.
6. S.P.O. S 12 882A, Lemass Memo on Labour Policy, June 1942.
7. Joseph Lee, 'Aspects of corporatist thought in Ireland: the Commission on Vocational Organisation, 1939-43', in A. Cosgrove and D. McCartney (eds.), *Studies in Irish History presented to R. Dudley Edwards* (Dublin, 1979), pp. 334 ff.
8. *Ibid.*, p. 329.
9. S.P.O. S 13 184A, Industry and Commerce memo, 26 February 1946.
10. Truman Library, F.H. Boland and Tom Murray, 'Oral History Interviews', in R.J. Raymond, *Ireland in the European Recovery Programme: 1947-53* (1978), unpaginated.
11. S.P.O. S 14 106D, External Affairs memo, 23 November 1948.
12. T.K. Whitaker, quoted in Fanning, *Finance*, p. 406.
13. UCD Archives, McGilligan Papers, P35B/75, Finance memo, 31 December 1948.
14. *Ibid.*
15. *Ibid.*
16. S.P.O. S 13 101B, Finance memo, 9 February 1953.
17. Maurice Moynihan, *Currency and Central Banking in Ireland 1922-60* (Dublin, 1975), pp. 394-9.
18. Fanning, *Finance*, p. 493.
19. Brian Girvin, 'Protectionism and Economic Development in Independent Ireland', pp. 301-2 (Ph.D. thesis, University College, Cork, 1986).
20. T.K. Whitaker, 'The Finance Attitude', *Administration*, 2, 3 (1953), re-printed in Basil Chubb and Patrick Lynch (eds.), *Economic Development and Planning* (Dublin, 1969), p. 43.
21. Fanning, *Finance*, p. 509.

Seán MacEntee (courtesy G.A. Duncan)

Gerard Sweetman (courtesy G.A. Duncan)

The Legacy of Economic Development: The Irish Economy 1960-1987

John Bradley

AN ECONOMY OR A NATION?

There is an understandable tendency for newly emerging countries to confuse national *autonomy* with national *sovereignty*. Sovereignty is the ability of a nation to act on its own rather than under the coercion of other nations.[1] National autonomy, on the other hand, describes the ability of a nation to attain its desired objectives, such as economic growth or full employment, if necessary through unilateral action. In the economic sphere the autonomy of small nations is heavily circumscribed and the recognition of this truth represents a wise exercise of national sovereignty. James Connolly's prophecy[2] that Irish independence might amount to a switching of flags and symbols was amply demonstrated in the first four decades of the new Irish state.[3]

Looking back at the first decades of a sovereign Ireland, its lack of economic autonomy is truly startling: the dominance of agriculture and the almost total dependence on the UK market the problems of functioning in a world dominated by protectionist policies and the need to copy these policies; the absence of an independent monetary authority; a conservative commercial class notable for its lack of progressive entrepreneurial instincts the partitioning of the country with its consequential political 'tunnel vision' and economic disruption; massive dislocation of international trade by a world war (euphemistically referred to in Ireland as the *Emergency*), which brought on a period of isolation which seems to have persisted, in one form or another, up to the late fifties.

A new age of economic planning was ushered in by *Economic*

128

Development and the *First Programme*. Economic policy over the period 1922–32 had been characterised by Irish adherence to the modified form of *laissez-faire* and free trade which prevailed in the UK at the same time. Orthodoxy in economic and financial matters prevailed as the new state established itself. The period 1932 to the mid-fifties had been marked by a drive to construct an indigenous Irish industrial base behind high tariff barriers. However, in relation to economic planning, political economists writing even as late as the fifties felt the need to justify state intervention in the economy against prevailing views hostile to such intervention.[5] Nevertheless, the economy from 1922–58 was not 'unplanned'. Anybody who has read accounts written by contemporary observers[6] will be aware of the state's role in creating such basic infrastructural business organisations as the ESB, Bord na Móna, Aer Lingus, etc. What was missing from that earlier period was the Keynesian language and inspiration which had characterised economic policy in the UK[7] and the US[8] from the immediate aftermath of the war, and the ability to take a broad overview of the supply potential of the economy. This latter notion of 'Ireland Inc' has always caused problems for Irish intellectuals, who were happier with more lofty concepts of Irishness. When these spiritual concepts were blended with Éamon de Valera's vision of frugal self-sufficiency, the outcome was unlikely to be a dynamic entrepreneural capitalism either in the public or private sectors.

The revolution in economic thinking, when it belatedly came, was swift and comprehensive. While in opposition during the fifties, Seán Lemass had immersed himself in new economic thinking and guided Fianna Fáil away from its Sinn Féin roots towards acceptance of a dependency on foreign capital and expertise and of an explicit Keynesian public policy framework. The progress of the parallel creative dynamic within the public sector has already been described in John McCarthy's essay. The dire state of the economy (low growth, massive emigration, balance of payments crises), the perceived failure of the policies of protection in bringing European-type growth to Ireland, and the failure of indigenous industries to reorient towards export markets from behind tariff barriers led directly to a fundamental policy revaluation, the details of which were codified and articulated in *Economic Development* and the *First Programme*. In this essay I review briefly the planning or programming process as it took root and propagated within Ireland, the particular form it took, its relationship to shifting views and fashions on economic theory and policy and its influence on Ireland's economic progress. A comprehensive evaluation of the complete Irish experience with economic planning has yet to be written, although excellent accounts of the origins and early stages are available.[9]

THE FIRST PROGRAMME: A NEW BEGINNING

From the publication of the *First Programme for Economic Expansion* in 1958 to the *Programme for National Recovery* in 1987, Irish economic policy-making has generally been formulated within the published guidelines of medium-term planning frameworks. We need not dwell too much on what precisely is a 'plan' or 'programme'. Dr Whitaker's definition will suffice: 'a coherent and comprehensive set of policies for economic and social development over a period of four to five years ahead'. He insists that any such plan 'must be consistent with the availability of resources and its various parts must be well integrated'. Great importance attaches to the notion of a plan, since it is 'the supreme policy document of the government'.[10]

More formally, a plan must have all of the following four elements. Firstly, an explicit choice of targets ranked in order of priority. The range of targets would typically include unemployment, inflation, the growth and level of real incomes. Secondly, a clear statement of the internal and external constraints facing the economy. Typical constraints would include the likely state of the world economy, the public sector's ability to borrow to finance its activities, and the nation's ability to 'pay its way' in the world (i.e. the balance of payments deficit).[11] Thirdly, the availability and selection of suitable policy instruments. Typical policy instruments include public sector employment, direct and indirect tax rates, income support schemes such as unemployment benefits and public sector investment. Finally, a thorough evaluation of the likely consequences of the proposed policy actions in attempting to achieve the stated targets without violating the known constraints.

Responsibility for drawing up plans and monitoring them has varied over the last three decades. Some have originated directly from within the Department of Finance; others from a special department with responsibility for planning functions and one originated, at least in part, from outside the civil service in an independent Planning Board. The somewhat ambivalent public and private attitudes to these plans has tended to conceal the important, if subliminal, role they play within the economy. In particular, their relationship to the annual budgetary process has always been left a little ambiguous. There is a sense in which the 'plan' represents what the government would ideally like to do, or what would be 'good' for the country in some normative and medium-term sense, but that the annual budget needs to be pragmatically flexible when buffeted by circumstances outside our control, or when political exigencies become too important to ignore, for example, near election time.

Economic Development and The First Programme

As we have seen in the earlier essays, *The First Programme* grew out of the crisis of the late fifties and, although motivated by a spirit of pragmatism, it represented the arrival of Keynesian macroeconomic thinking and policies in Ireland. Of crucial importance was the role staked out for the public authorities in the planning process. Speaking in 1961, Seán Lemass asserted that,

> In Irish economic development, the role of the Government is predominant. Nobody believes that, in the circumstances of this country, economic progress on the scale which is needed is likely to be realised otherwise than through the medium of a strong and sound Government policy directed to that result. . . . The vast dynamic of growth which is inherent in free private enterprise cannot be fully availed of without Government drive and leadership.[12]

However, there were differences between the enthusiastic, explicit

131

and unbridled Keynesianism of Lemass and the more guarded and exacting approach of Whitaker. For example, Whitaker's critique of Keynesian policy prescriptions as applied to a small exposed economy like Ireland and his insistence on the primacy of what we would today call 'supply-side' policies, were prophetic, particularly in the light of the subsequent explosive growth of the public sector.[13] Nevertheless, the portrayal of Whitaker as an ideological right-wing free-marketer[14] is far off the mark given the documented record of his commitment to the need for state intervention to manage aggregate demand and not leave the economy to the mercy of market forces.[15]

Certain aspects of *The First Programme* are of interest from the point of view of the subsequent development of planning in Ireland. Nature abhors a vacuum and *Economic Development* filled such a vacuum. It is to the credit of the politicians of the day that, however reluctantly, they acknowledged this and shared the limelight with its author, the head of the civil service. Also, we have become so used to the passionless language of later plans that the honesty, directness and clarity of *Economic Development* should be remembered.[16]

The 'psychological' aspect was emphasised in *Economic Development*, although the real meaning of this remains obscure. Clearly the programme was intended to be the vehicle of decisive political action, not a substitute for it, and from Lemass's leadership this political action was forthcoming. The population recognised this new sense of direction and purpose and responded positively to its ambition and vision. A justification for the duration of the plan (1959-63) was that the traditional budgetary year was too short a time frame for strategic policy-making. A much broader framework was needed. However, planning over a long time horizon brought its own problems. For example, the expectation that the agriculture sector would provide the 'engine' of growth proved to be wrong, and that role was played by the new burgeoning foreign-owned industrial sector. Much attention was paid to the domestic sources of capital financing and the necessity to increase domestic savings. In the event, the large inflows of private foreign capital eased the domestic financing constraint.[17] Even the projections of public capital spending were exceeded, so the plan did not serve well as a guide to the evolution of a key set of its own policy instruments! Overall economic growth of 23 per cent for the duration of the programme (1959–63) exceeded the 'target' of 11 per cent. Understandably, this was not the subject of criticism. Quite the reverse! However, it opened up a gap between the planner's projections and the outturn which was ill-understood. This would return to haunt the policy-makers in later programmes.

THE DECLINE OF PLANNING

The Second and Third Programmes: 1964–72
The loose framework of the *First Programme* contrasts sharply with the complex methodological structures of the *Second* and *Third*. Developments in national accounting statistics, partially initiated as a result of the *First Programme*, provided a comprehensive national accounting framework which imposed a formal discipline and consistency which was lacking in the earlier plan. A further innovation in these programmes was the use of formal economic techniques, including a mathematical model of the Irish economy, to perform economic computations and consistency checks. The target of both later programmes was to obtain a profile of the Irish economy at a specified terminal date (1970 for the *Second*, 1973 for the *Third*), which reflected the highest growth rate which could be achieved in the light of 'policy possibilities, the probable development of the external environment and resource availability'. In both programmes, a target aggregate growth rate of approximately 4 per cent for national output was broken down into internally consistent sub-targets for the sectoral components.[18]

It may seem paradoxical to describe this period as representing the decline of planning. However, the very ambition of the planners to quantify at a high level of sectoral and institutional detail contained the seeds of its own destruction. With hindsight, the methodological underpinnings of the plans were flawed and the economic tools of analysis inadequate to capture the market dynamics of a rapidly developing small and open economy.[19]

As unfolding international and domestic developments rendered the projections of the *Third Programme* increasingly unrealistic, the planning process was gradually abandoned. Paradoxically, during the most turbulent period of the post-war world economy, in the lead into, and immediate aftermath of, the first OPEC oil price crisis, there was no plan or programme formally in place. The extent of planning's fall from grace is captured by the remarks of the coalition government's Minister for Finance, Mr Richie Ryan, in the 1975 budget speech, when he said: 'Of all the tasks which could engage my attention, the least realistic would be the publication of a medium or long-term economic plan based on irrelevancies in the past, hunches as to the present and clairvoyance as to the future'. Such an approach 'would not be meaningful in the context of the unsettled world situation'. As a result of this lack of foresight, a policy change of crucial future consequence went through without a comprehensive economic analysis of its medium-term consequences. Starting in 1972, the government planned for, and incurred, deficits on its current account and these deficits on day-to-day expenses were financed by borrowing, mainly abroad.

In summary, the first phase of economic planning in Ireland covered the period 1958 to the end of the sixties. The extent to which the obvious increased growth of the Irish economy, towards rates prevailing in mainland Europe, was a result of these programmes remains an open issue. Neary concludes rather pessimistically that 'the programmes were not really the cause of the economic progress which occurred in the 1960s and the early 1970s. They accompanied it and charted its course'. He surmised that it was the new outward-looking policies towards foreign trade and investment, rather than the programmes, which caused the economy to take off.[20] However, this is a somewhat artificial distinction since the policy of openness, together with the tax and capital incentives designed to attract foreign industry, were fundamental parts of the programmes.

Planning Briefly Revived: National Development 1977-1980
The decade of the seventies was characterised by fluctuations in
the world economy of a kind which had not been experienced
in peacetime since the thirties. Even with the wisest and most
prudent fiscal and monetary policies it would have been impossible to protect the Irish economy fully from the world-wide
recession. This period also marked the onset of an extensive dis-
enchantment with the Keynesian policies of state intervention
and demand management which had been widely used in the
fifties and sixties in most western economies. Instead in market-
oriented economics revived and, towards the end of the seventies,
governments in the western world came to power with political
mandates to roll back state interference and to deregulate and
liberalise markets. It is truly ironic that it was in just such a hostile international intellectual climate that economic planning was
revived here in Ireland.

Whereas the *First Programme* originated from within the civil
service in a relatively non-political way, the seeds of a revival of
economic planning over the period 1977 to the end of the decade
came from a party political manifesto. On entering into office
in June 1977, the new Fianna Fáil administration set up a Department of Economic Planning and Development, a decision which
was opposed strongly by the author of *Economic Development*
in his role as Senator.[21] Two publications in particular serve to
characterise this period: *National Development 1977-1980* and
Development for Full Employment. Did these documents have
all the necessary attributes of a 'plan'? They were explicit and
ambitious in terms of their growth and unemployment targets,
and their massive use of public expenditure increases and tax
cuts. On the analysis of the constraints facing the achievement
of these targets, the planners could not use the excuse of earlier
workers – that of a dearth of quantitative knowledge about the
functioning and properties of the economy. *Even* within a
Keynesian framework of analysis, the limited influence of state
intervention in a small open economy was well known by this
time. On the evaluation of the consequences of policy actions,
the work reported in the published documents was excessively

optimistic, unconvincing and singularly failed to build any consensus within the pool of economic experts in the country.[22] Consequently, the planning process, which had started out in 1958 commanding wide professional and popular consensus, became the subject of much public and political controversy.

PLANNING WITH BINDING CONSTRAINTS: 1981–1987

The second OPEC oil price crisis of 1979 spelled the end of the final period of 'optimistic' planning which had started in 1977. It also ushered in a period of political instability, there being three general elections between June 1981 and December 1982. *The Way Forward*, published in October 1982 marked the start of a transition to a more sombre and realistic appraisal of the nature of the new constraints facing policy-makers in Ireland. It emphasised the economic problems besetting most developed countries: slower growth, high inflation, high unemployment and balance of payments deficits. However, quite optimistic assumptions were made about the future international environment and within these assumptions it planned to eliminate the now burgeoning current deficit completely by 1986. The instruments selected included a combination of expenditure cuts (mainly through public sector employment cuts combined with wage moderation) and charges for state services. Off-setting positive employment growth was to come from manufacturing and services through a process of wage moderation. Although targets and instruments were clearly isolated in the plan, its evaluation of the constraints – both political and economic – facing the achievement of these targets proved unduly optimistic. In the event, the general election called immediately after the publication of *The Way Forward* returned a new administration, and a centre-left coalition government of Fine Gael and Labour was formed.

The plan which covered the term of the coalition administration of 1982–86 came in two stages: the *Proposals For Plan 1984–87* in April 1984 and *Building on Reality* in the Autumn of 1984. The National Planning Board was established in March

1983 with the task of drafting a medium-term programme for the economy within which short-term economic planning could proceed. The Board consisted of seven members, all from outside the civil service, two of whom were professional economists, and had a director and secretariate of professional economists. Their report, a comprehensive document containing 241 recommendations, was used as an input into the production of the actual government plan, *Building on Reality*, which was drawn up within the Departments of Finance and of the Taoiseach. This latter document, beneath its optimistic rhetoric, was probably the most sober planning document of all published in the period since 1958. Essentially, it was a manifesto on how to deal with the burgeoning fiscal imbalance without being seen to deflate the economy excessively, a process roughly akin to squaring the circle. It was perceived as a political rather than as an economic document and, in the absence of political consensus on economic policy (to some degree even within the coalition government itself), it was the subject of much controversy over its period of operation. With an unfavourable international climate (in particular, historically high real interest rates) the political will seems to have been lacking to wind back the large-scale state involvement in the economy and reduce a level of state indebtedness which has reached crisis proportions. During these years the political air was filled with mutual and bitter recriminations.

After a change of government in February 1987, the plan in operation at present, the *Programme for National Recovery*, was published in October 1987, and included a detailed pay agreement for both public and private sectors for the period to 1990. By this time, the precarious size and nature of the fiscal imbalance was acknowledged to be so serious that major and immediate surgery was needed. The overriding objective had become the stabilisation of the inexorably rising debt-GNP ratio so as to break out of a vicious circle of intensifying debt, an increasingly intolerable tax burden on wage income, loss of international competitiveness and spiralling unemployment and emigration. However, the fundamental ambivalence that characterises Irish plans endured. The *Programme* was relatively silent on the draconian expenditure cuts being contemplated by the government, the details of which were published *after* the plan in the public expenditure *Estimates* for the year 1988. This nice sense of timing ensured that a crucial element of the *Programme*, the national wage agreement, could be concluded with the Trades Unions before the nature and extent of the cuts were widely understood.

MEANWHILE, BACK AT THE ECONOMY

How did the Irish economy fare over the thirty-year era of economic planning? Were we promoted or relegated in the league of international comparisons? If we were promoted, was it because of, or in spite of, the activities of the economic planners?

Two key economic measures capture the overall story of the Irish economy over the last thirty years: real growth and the unemployment rate. Figure 1 shows the growth rate of real gross national product (GNP) since 1958 while Figure 2 shows the unemployment rate. By the standards of the late seventies and the decade following *Economic Development* was truly a golden age of sustained high growth and low unemployment. However, just as Lemass's rising tide lifted all domestic ships, could it be that there was an international rising tide? In other words, did Ireland manage to grow *relative* to other similar European countries? Tables 1 and 2 show how Ireland fared relative to Denmark, Belgium, Norway and Finland, four of the club of small rich countries. All five countries had broadly similar growth rates on average. Hence, while Ireland singularly failed to converge upwards towards the *per-capita* GDP of its initially richer neighbours, neither was there any systematic tendency towards further deterioration. Turning to comparative unemployment, Figure 3 shows Ireland's unemployment rate in 1985 compared with the rest of the OECD countries.

So, Ireland not only failed to catch up with the wealthier European countries but by 1985 it had the second highest rate of unemployment in the OECD (after Spain). However, behind this simplistic comparison in terms of aggregate growth and unemployment lay good and bad developments. For example, the industrial sector grew while the importance of agriculture declined (Figure 4) and within industry the modern sector came to dominate the traditional sector[23] (Figure 5). Not only did exports from the modern industrial sector outstrip agricultural exports (Figure 6) but also their destinations were considerably more diversified than in the early decades of the state when the UK was totally dominant (Figure 7).

All these were good developments and were foreseen in the economic plans. However, there was a dark side to the story. A large proportion of net employment creation was in the public sector (Figure 8) and total public expenditure steadily monopolised a growing proportion of GNP. With few exceptions taxes grew steadily every year as a proportion of GNP (Figure 9). Yet even as she became heavily taxed, Ireland simultaneously became heavily indebted, and the total national debt as a percentage of GNP reached the dizzy heights of 150 per cent in 1987. The really worrying aspect of this debt was that a sizable fraction of it (over a third by 1987) had been borrowed from foreigners, the interest payments on which represented a net loss to the economy.

Finally, a feature of industrial growth in recent years has been an increasingly high level of profit repatriation by multinational industries producing in Ireland. Such outflows are a normal feature associated with foreign direct investment. However, multinational high-technology firms that have located in Ireland over the last few decades tend to be intensive in terms of capital and research, source most of their inputs abroad, have relatively weak downstream links with the rest of the economy and repatriate the major part of their profits. Public policy has not yet succeeded in building on existing Irish industrial strengths to develop firms which will generate and retain a greater portion of added-value within the economy. The dilemma of policy remains particularly acute: low wage costs and an adequate supply of trained workers are a key element serving to attract industry to Ireland but the low downstream linkage and the high rate of profit repatriation means that the domestic wage bill is the main benefit received from such activity. The foreign-led industrial growth strategy developed into, at best, a *zero-sum* game (i.e. of little *net* benefit to the economy).

THE LESSONS OF ECONOMIC PLANNING

Any detailed attempt to attribute success or failure to individual plans would be impossible. In the first place, it is the annual budget that actually implements government economic policy decisions, not the plan. The budgetary process involves a multitude of policy instruments, complex timing of changes, is spread over the whole year and embodies a high degree of continuity with past policies.[24] In addition, the assumptions made *ex ante* in the plans about, say, the international environment may not be realised *ex post*. Irish planners can hardly be blamed for not forecasting the Yom Kippur and Iran-Iraq wars, the depth and duration of the recession of the early eighties or the extraordinary bad weather of 1985/6. These assumptions are made by both politicians and public servants. Politicians are usually, by nature and selection, assertive, optimistic people. Public servants in general are calculating risk-averse pessimists, while those in the Department of Finance are expected to be downright gloomy Scrooges. Out of the creative tensions between these different personalities our plans are born and the best plans have been those which achieve an elusive balance. The *First Programme* had this balance. The plans of the 1977-80 period had not.

To some extent, the dominant features of Irish economic plans (in particular, the nature and degree of state activity) arose from their broadly accepted Keynesian intellectual underpinnings. One of the results of the Keynesian revolution had been to play down the significance of resource allocation issues and to stress the limitations rather than the uses of markets. However, today we are faced with a situation where economic planning by the state is unfashionable and no longer holds the 'high ground' of national concensus. Past planning experience has taught us that in a small open economy the ability of state intervention to achieve policy goals is extremely circumscribed, no matter what view of economics one holds. More recent developments have broken with the previous Keynesian tradition and the underpinnings of present policies and plans have taken on aspects of a more market-oriented economics.

The concept of the market is central to economics since in a market economy this is the mechanism by which scarce resources are efficiently allocated. Economists can be classified in terms of their attitudes to market forces and to market intervention by governments. A free-marketer holds that the role of governments should be restricted to setting the ground-rules or laws required by the system of private property. The opposite Marxist position replaces markets by a system of central planning where resources are entirely allocated by government *diktat*. What is interesting about the Irish political party system, shaped as it was by the civil war, is that it bears little resemblance to the right/left or conservative/socialist divide that characterised British and European politics in the twentieth century.[25] The main Irish political parties try to keep to the ideological centre and the closer they are to office the more they consolidate a moderate centre position in their actions. During a period of strong economic growth, policy changes are less controversial since it is easier to divide up a growing cake than a fixed or shrinking one. The Lemassian *dictum* of 'rising tides' eases political tension.

The 1987 general election took place after a period of unprecedented stagnation of growth, historically high unemployment and chronic imbalances in the state finances. While all political parties acknowledged these problems, they disagreed strongly on apportioning blame and proposing solutions. If the 1951 election has been described as the first Irish 'pork barrel' election,[26] 1987 could be characterised as the first ideological one, where the previous economic consensus showed a distinct tendency to break down in the face of unpleasant policy choices.

Through a Glass Darkly

In looking ahead to the next Irish economic plan, both our experience of the past and that of other small European states is relevant.[27] Almost without exception, the small European states have carved a path between liberalism and statism, and have evolved towards indirect forms of economic control. What characterises the economic and political experience of small European states and sets them apart from the large industrial countries is the 'premise' of their planning efforts: adaptation to external market forces. They have generally come to find detailed comprehensive sectoral planning efforts increasingly inapplicable, simply because of the openness and vulnerability of their economies. Their problem is one of selecting the devices of planning that are in harmony with their social objectives. Hence, the *rationale* for state intervention depends on the ability or otherwise of market forces to yield results consistent with these social objectives. Because of their lack of autonomy, their strategy must be flexible, reactive and incremental. They cannot oppose adverse change by shifting its costs to others abroad. Instead, they must continually improvise in living with change. The success or otherwise of this continual process of improvisation will depend in large part on the efficiency with which they learn the lessons of their previous planning efforts.

Is the time ripe for the emergence of a new *Economic Development* to map out Ireland's future over the next thirty years? The world is a much more complex place now than it was in 1958 and every aspect of economic and cultural life in Ireland is exposed to international influences to an extent that would have seemed unbelievable to the planners of that earlier period. The imminent arrival of the Single European Market represents the logical culmination of this trend. It would be wise to assume that these changes are irreversible. In addition, attitudes to public sector intervention in the economy have changed, not only in the western world but also in the centrally planned economies of Eastern Europe and China. For better or for worse, the previous spirit of what David Henderson has called 'unreflecting centralism'[28] (i.e. the readiness to assume that decisions have to be taken by governments and that governments can pick winners) has faded and been replaced by a willingness to rely on a more Darwinian outcome based on the survival of the fittest in the cut and thrust of market forces. If Seán Lemass and Dr Whitaker were the popular heroes of the sixties and seventies, this role is now played by prominent personalities from the business world.

The core of any new *Economic Development* will be the manner in which it can reconcile the twin goals of efficiency and equity. For economic policy to be successful it must be hard-headed but soft-hearted.[29] But the very success of the policies of the past thirty years has given rise to what Mancur Olson calls 'distributional coalitions', powerful lobbies among employers, employees and the state who are more oriented to struggles over the distribution of income and wealth than to the production of additional output.[30] Consequently, it has become increasingly difficult in Ireland to negotiate and implement policies where there are winners and losers, and the sense of frustration this engenders risks leading to a breakdown of the already fragile consensus between the social partners. The single most important criterion of success of any new *Economic Development* will be the extent to which it can chart the way towards the elimination of the social evil of mass unemployment, probably the root cause of much of the social inequality in Ireland today. Nothing in the last thirty years, either here or abroad, convincingly demonstrates that this task will be accomplished without active and fruitful co-operation between the private and state sectors.

Table 1. *Average Growth Rates of Gross Domestic Product Per Capita*

	1951–73	1974–85	1951–85
Belgium	3.6	1.9	3.0
Denmark	3.1	2.0	2.8
Finland	4.2	2.3	3.6
Norway	3.3	3.9	3.5
Ireland	3.0	3.9	3.5

Table 2. *Gross Domestic Product Per Capita Relative to Ireland*

	1950	1973	1985
Belgium	1.7	1.9	1.9
Denmark	2.1	2.2	2.1
Finland	1.4	1.8	1.8
Norway	1.9	2.0	2.4

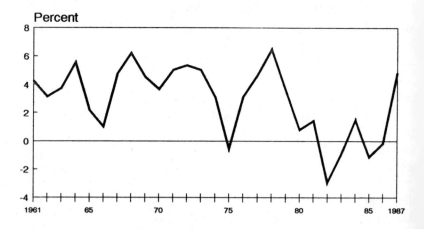

Figure 1. *Growth Rate of Real GNP*

144

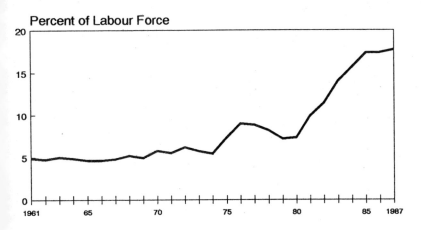

Figure 2. *Rate of Unemployment*

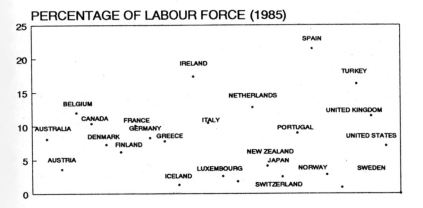

Figure 3. *OECD Unemployment Rates*

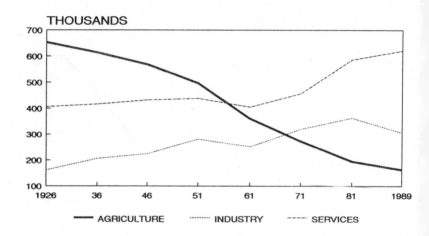

Figure 4. *Sectoral Employment: 1926-1989*

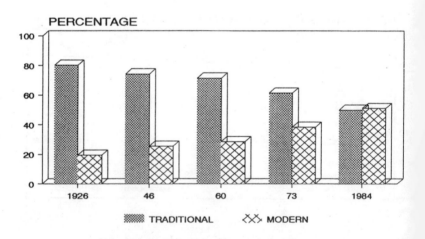

Figure 5. *Shares of Manufacturing Employment*

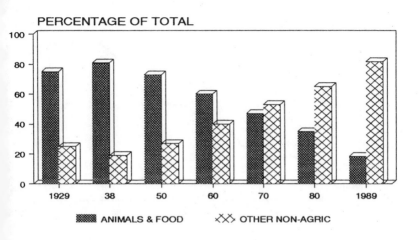

Figure 6. *Composition of Irish Exports*

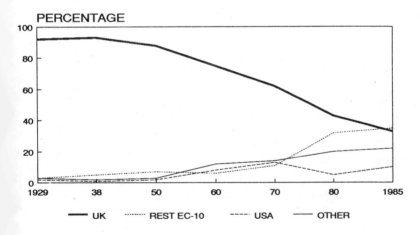

Figure 7. *Irish Exports: Geographical Destination*

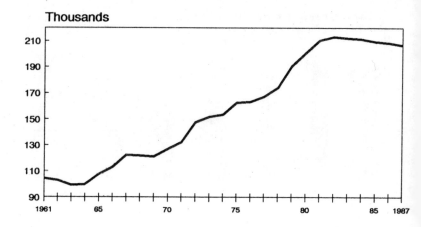

Figure 8. *Public Sector Employment*

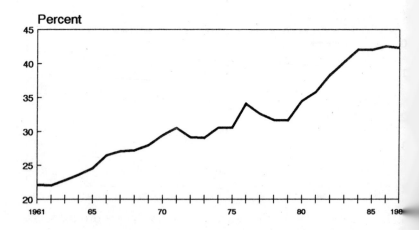

Figure 9. *Total Taxes as Percent of GNP*

NOTES

1. To take a modern example, Ireland could leave the EC but would have to suffer some unpleasant adjustments if she did so.
2. 'If you remove the English army to-morrow and hoist the green flag over Dublin Castle, . . . England would still rule you. She would rule you through her capitalists, through her landlords, through her financiers, through the whole array of commercial and individualist institutions she has planted in this country . . .;' James Connolly, *Socialism and Nationalism* (Dublin, 1948). This article first appeared in 1897.
3. Ronan Fanning, *The Irish Department of Finance 1922–58* (Dublin, 1978).
4. This sense of isolation after the Second World War, and the difficulties in overcoming it, are documented in Miriam Hederman's book *The Road to Europe: Irish Attitudes 1948–61* (Dublin, 1983).
5. F.C. King, 'Drifting to Absolutism', *Journal of the Statistical and Social Inquiry Society*, 1952; Patrick Lynch, 'The Economist and Public Policy', *Studies*, Autumn, 1953.
6. For example, C.S. Andrews, *A Man of No Property* (Cork, 1981).
7. W.H. Beveridge, *Full Employment in a Free Society* (London, 1944).
8. Employment Act, 1946.
9. B. Chubb and P. Lynch, *Economic Development and Planning* (Dublin, 1969); R. Fanning, *The Irish Department of Finance, 1922–58* (Dublin, 1968); O. Katsiaouni, 'Planning in a Small Economy: The Republic of Ireland', *Journal of the Statistical and Social Inquiry Society of Ireland*, vol. xxiii, 1977.
10. T.K. Whitaker, 'The Department of Economic Planning and Development', *Interests* (Dublin, 1983).
11. Constraints can, alas, mutate into binding targets. A decade-and-a-half of public sector profligacy has resulted in the debt/GNP ratio making this transition!
12. Quoted in P. Bew and H. Patterson, *Seán Lemass and the Making of Modern Ireland 1946–66* (Dublin, 1982).
13. For example, the section of his Statistical and Social Inquiry Society paper in 1956 dealing with the limited role of the Keynesian multiplier in a small open economy.
14. Bew and Patterson, *op. cit.*
15. R. Fanning, *The Irish Department of Finance, 1922–58* (Dublin, 1978).
16. In the light of present-day sensitivities to the nuances of every interest group, a certain political naïvety characterised the references to 'the virtual satisfaction of needs' in housing and other forms of social investment. This was an attitude which would be carefully excised from all future plans.

149

17. In part these capital flows were the result of the process of dismantling trade barriers, which was well under way even before the publication of the *First Programme*.

18. The 4 per cent growth rate chosen was never justified satisfactorily, but was broadly in line with projected OECD growth rates.

19. A pool of applicable empirical research was developing, in the then newly founded Economic & Social Research Institute and elsewhere. However, it is worth remembering that the *Economic & Social Review*, the main vehicle of economic publication in Ireland (together with the older *Journal of the Statistical & Social Inquiry Society*) was not founded until 1969. The first full-scale Keynesian macroeconomic model for Ireland was not constructed until 1966, but was not available for operational use by policy-makers.

20. J.P. Neary, 'The failure of Irish Nationalism', in *Ireland: Dependence and Independence, The Crane Bag*, vol. 8, 1984.

21. T.K. Whitaker, 'The Department of Economic Planning and Development', *Interests* (Dublin, 1983).

22. Whether this failure was political or economic in nature remains an open question. Given the Irish propensity towards imitative social behaviour, perhaps if Margaret Thatcher and Ronald Reagan had come to power three years earlier all would have been different.

23. The traditional sector includes food, drink, clothing, footwear, etc. while the modern sector includes chemicals, engineering, metal products, etc.

24. For the technically minded, a detailed analysis of the budgets of the 1967–80 period is provided in Bradley *et al.*, *Medium-Term Analysis of Fiscal Policy in Ireland* (Dublin, Research Paper No. 122, 1985).

25. The historian, Ronan Fanning, writing about the Labour Party's stance of principled neutrality in response to the Treaty split of 1922, commented: 'Labour, by standing aside on what became and remained the great divide in Irish politics, recognised the continuing irrelevance of socialism for the majority of Irish voters and effectively admitted that Ireland, as Engels had remarked to Marx fifty years earlier, "still remains the Holy Isle whose aspirations must on no account be mixed with the profane class struggles of the rest of the sinful world" ' (R. Fanning, *Independent Ireland* (Dublin, 1983).

26. R. Fanning, *op. cit.*

27. P. Katzenstein, *Small States in World Markets* (Ithaca, 1985).

28. D. Henderson, *Innocence and Design: the Influence of Economic Ideas on Policy* (Oxford, 1985).

29. A. Blinder, *Hard Heads and Soft Hearts: Tough-Minded Economics for a Just Society* (New York, 1987).

30. Mancur Olson, *The Rise and Decline of Nations* (New Haven, 1982).

Eamon de Valera (courtesy G.A. Duncan)

Other Toms, Other Moores

Bernard Share

One evening in early March 1953 an enterprising Trinity College student took possession of the plastic Bowl of Light which ornamented a concrete water trough (otherwise known as the Tomb of the Unknown Gurrier) on Dublin's O'Connell Bridge, and hurled it into the Liffey. Few lamented its immersion — the cartoon in the *Irish Times* depicted two officials concluding that it was the work either of the Animal Gang or the two-year-old Arts Council — but the attitude of Trinity's undergraduate magazine, *TCD*, was surprisingly censorious. 'There has been a regrettable outbreak of thoroughly bad behaviour in Dublin recently', it admonished, 'and Trinity students have played a large part in it. To say that the two Tóstal ornaments . . . were not artistically pleasing is no excuse for the drunken participation of Trinity students in that destruction. Fortunately, Dubliners bark more sharply than they bite, or we might have seen a repetition of the riots of 1859 and 1945.'

The incident in 1945 when pro-British students burned an Irish flag in the course of celebrations marking the end of the War in Europe was, in the early fifties, still a ponderable factor in the College's relations with the city without its walls. The flood of ex-service students, many of them with no roots in Ireland ('Why did you come to Trinity?' — 'I couldn't get into Sheffield') had, if anything, increased the isolation of an institution already distanced from the main preoccupations of Irish life by the ban on the attendance of Catholics, imposed by the Archbishop of Dublin, Dr McQuaid. In June 1950 the Board, Trinity's governing body, directed that a debate: 'That this House prefers orange to green', be held in camera. Éamon de Valera, addressing a meet-

152

ing of the University Philosophical Society on 3 March 1949, had confronted, and quietly downfaced, an audience composed largely of vociferous Northern unionists. He was appearing in an unfamiliar – both to himself and his audience – capacity as leader of the opposition.

The general election of February 1948 had resulted in a good deal more than a simple change in political leadership after sixteen years of Fianna Fáil rule. The Emergency period and the years immediately following had marked something of a stasis in Irish society, preserving a fabric that had altered little since the foundation of the State. With the Coalition assuming power against the background of the final dispelling of the clouds of war, and new moves towards the reorientation of Europe, things began, however tentatively, to change. The first moves were negative: the ritual demolition, in the name of financial rectitude, of several edifices Fianna Fáil had been in the course of constructing – the Aer Lingus transatlantic service, the Radio Éireann long wave transmitter. Queen Victoria departed from the lawn of Leinster House, symbolically clearing the air for the repeal of the External Relations Act, announced in September 1948 a move seen by many, not all of them in the North, as copper-fastening Partition. That institution had, with the change of government, come under heavy attack with the setting up of the Mansion House Committee and the publication, overseen by a young official at the Department of External Affairs, Conor Cruise O'Brien, of a series of propaganda booklets alleging discrimination and gerrymandering on the part of the Northern majority. One of these, *Discrimination – a study in injustice to a minority*, contrasted, under a heading 'COMPARE THESE', Statements by Spokesmen of the Minority in Free Ireland' printed in green) with 'Statements by Spokesmen of the Minority in Occupied Ireland' (printed in orange). The Anti-Partition Conference under whose imprimatur this material was issued was described as 'All-Party', but individual initiative was by no means lacking. 'For some reason', wrote Dónal Barrington, 'after he fell from power in 1948, Mr de Valera abandoned his former policy of silence, and made Partition the central issue on the Irish political stage. Mr Costello [the new Taoiseach] decided not to be outdone, and Mr MacBride wished to do something dynamic. . . .'

MacBride's dynamism was evidenced also in other areas. In three lectures in Dublin in 1949 under the auspices of his success-ful new party, Clann na Poblachta, he attacked emigration, the link with sterling (recently devalued by the British) and 'the evil of any portion of land remaining unproductive', advocating, in respect of the latter condition, a major afforestation programme. He, or the government in which he served, was responsible for the setting up of the Irish News Agency, the Industrial Develop-ment Authority and the Cultural Relations Committee of the Department of External Affairs – all designed to make contacts with and have influence upon the outside world in both the eco-nomic and cultural spheres.

There were, and probably still are, two views as to the effect of the isolation imposed by wartime neutrality on the ethos of the country, particularly as it related to its cultural development. One is the view, fostered by the British and those in sympathy with them, that in remaining a non-belligerent, Ireland had cut herself off to a fatal degree from the mainstream, wherever that was considered to run. The other suggested that the country had benefited from an enforced recourse to self-reliance and an independent policy, an attitude voiced by an editorial in *The Bell* of March 1954: 'The war years . . . with their necessary isolation produced a curious liveliness of interest about the phenomena of Irish life. That kind of national, introvert curiosity', it went on to suggest, 'has diminished a little. . . .'

That dimunition was nowhere more evident than in the literary sphere. Though Yeats had died in France in 1939, the formal end of the era which he represented was signalled by the arrival in Galway on 17 September 1948 of the naval corvette *Macha* bearing his remains for reburial in Drumcliffe. 'It is fitting that a country which takes pride in its poets should accord him national respect', said the *Irish Times* leader on the same day; but for the new generation of Irish writers that same national respect was a commodity which appeared to be accorded only very grudgingly if at all. 'Ireland offers three prospects to the young writer o promise', wrote John Ryan in 1951: 'poverty, obscurity and hatred'. Ryan had founded, in 1949, the magazine *Envoy*, which, for the term of its brief existence – it closed in July 1951 – was to provide the focus for this genre of protest, particularly in the person and *persona* of Patrick Kavanagh. The journal assembled a formidable array of talent: not only those domestically-based writers then established or coming into prominence, such as Anthony Cronin, Valentin Irenmonger (the poetry editor), Brendan Behan, Aidan Higgins, Benedict Kiely, Donat O'Donnell (Conor Cruise O'Brien), Myles na gCopaleen (to whom this essay is indebted for its title) and others, but expatriates or returning expatriates such as Samuel Beckett and Francis Stuart. 'An Irish journal is like a sortie from a besieged city. Its effects cannot be measured by its duration', said Hubert Butler in its senior contemporary, *The Bell*; but if this was demonstrably true of *Envoy*, the sorties were to some extent circumscribed in their effectiveness by an uncertainty as to who, and where, was the enemy. Kavanagh himself, in his regular *Diary*, was inclined to fight on two fronts, at one moment opting for the purity of native (i.e. Catholic) inspiration undefiled, at another lamenting the provincialism of the Irish literary scene. David Marcus and Terence Smith, editors of *Irish Writing*, founded in Cork in 1946, inclined to the latter position in the issue number 20/21 (November 1952): 'In much of the "creative" writing coming from Ireland today there is more than a suggestion of over-tillage'. But two issues later, in the special An Tóstal number, they were not so sure: 'Few would deny the existence of a certain spiritual isolationism in Ireland today. What remains less certain is the question as to whether it is a curse or a blessing'. Whilst this dilemma was to manifest itself repeatedly in the thinking and discussion of the decade 1948-58 Anthony Cronin perceived the malaise, in its literary context, in more straightforward terms.

> There is at present a disquieting lull in creative activity in Ireland, [he wrote in September 1951] and a lack of creative vitality in the generations now in their twenties or early thirties, giving cause for the fear that what the editor [Peadar O'Donnell of *The Bell*] calls 'the Irish School of writing' may disappear altogether – or, as I would

prefer to say, Ireland may be left altogether without a contemporary literature.

A similar view was expressed in more general terms by Fr Burke Savage, SJ, introducing a series of essays under the title 'Ireland Tomorrow' in *Studies* (1955). He referred to '. . . the common undertone running through these pages: the plea for a more creative outlook. It is at least arguable that this creative outlook is lacking because of our failure to fashion a satisfying ideal for our people.'

The prevailing atmosphere of disillusionment had its origins, however, as much in practical as in spiritual deficiencies. In 1950, 36,000 emigrants, largely skilled construction workers in Britain, were induced to return by the promise of jobs which failed to materialise. Most university students assumed, rightly, that upon graduation they would have no option but to emigrate. Paul Blanchard's book, *The Vanishing Irish*, envisaged a doomsday situation in which many were prepared to acquiesce. Neil O'Kennedy, drawing as 'NO'K' in the *Irish Times*, encapsulated the situation. One unsuccessful entrant for the Abbey playwrighting competition tells another: 'I suppose my dramatisation of "The Vanishing Irish" was a bit avant-garde: just a set – no actors'. The same piquantly predicative concept (Godot was still awaited) surfaced in Thomas Hogan's (Thomas Woods) theatre review in the March 1950 issue of *Envoy*:

> Among my unwritten plays there are two designed for which I thought would have been the finish up of the tradition of economic and relatively motionless acting. One is to be performed with a black curtain across the proscenium arch with holes cut in it so that the actors can shout their lines unwinkingly at the audience. The other presents possibly insuperable technical difficulties for it is designed for no actors at all.

There were several other variations of this generalised expectation that the last man to leave Ireland would shortly be putting out the light. It was said, and believed, that de Valera's somewhat late awakening to the problems of emigration was occasioned by a cartoon in *Dublin Opinion*. In the absence of popular economists to explain the problem away — their role as the arbiters of the national destiny lay in the future — the drain was felt as a corporate shame, lacking even the consolation of the latter-day cynicism that as many people as possible were being induced to leave, to make Ireland a more comfortable place for her 'yuppies' to live in. MacBride, in his 1949 lecture, put it formally:

> This problem of emigration and under-employment is damaging to the social structure of the Christian State as we conceive it.... More often than not, those who are forced to emigrate are immature physically and mentally and are ill-equipped for the impact of the conditions that prevail in the industrial centres where they go in search of work.

For Patrick Kavanagh and his brother Peter, who wrote, edited and produced thirteen issues of *Kavanagh's Weekly* in 1952, the true motivation behind this mass exodus was easily discernible: 'Why are the people leaving the countryside in their thousands? They go to England where conditions are extremely bad. What they are seeking is the enthusiasm for life'.

Life — more usually with the capital initial — was presented by these two supreme begrudgers as the *terminus ad quem*, though its precise definition ('one must beware of being too logical about anything') was to prove elusive. The Kavanaghs evinced total impartiality in attacking everything and everybody in Ireland failing to measure up to their exacting, if evasive, standard and capable of being assembled within the bounds of the provincial wilderness dominated by 'Ireland's Four Pillars of Wisdom — let me name them right away: The Christian Brothers, Croke Park, Radio Iran [sic], The Queen's Theatre'. (The Abbey having burnt down in 1951 — an event in which the Kavanaghs saw the hand of God — the company was playing in the latter premises.) Whilst *Kavanagh's Weekly* exemplified the contemporary blend of begrudgery and national inferiority complex in what might be termed its purest form, its sweeping castigations of the perceived mediocrity of Irish society contained just sufficient of a germ of practical truth to cause some of the mud to stick. The furore aroused by an article on Ireland, in similar vein, by Seán Ó Faoláin in the US magazine *Holiday* suggested that even the upholders of the *status quo*, a comfortable majority, felt a certain uneasiness about a community which, having declared itself to be a republic in a move which savoured of the expedient, both in the form of its announcement and the manner of its celebration (the salute of guns on Sunday, 17 April 1949 was muffled in more senses than one), was experiencing difficulty in formulating its identity as something other than non-British. 'This week Dublin Castle will fall again to the Gael', wrote the *Sunday Press* on the occasion of the inauguration in 1952 of Seán T. O'Kelly for his second presidential term:

> Six silver trumpets flashing in the lights, a stirring of old banners on the walls. . . . The ghost of Empire will laugh its bitter laugh, that in this hurdle fort – for seven centuries the centre of royal military power, the very core of English rule – Irishmen should gather to recognise THEIR head of THEIR State.

The London *Observer*, in a profile, looked forward to the President's second term:

> The Ulster question may not forever be the main item of foreign policy, the secure sense of being an island beyond an island must finally give way to an awareness of modern strategic and ideological realities, and the social progress of the people will probably bulk increasingly in the action of political life here as elsewhere. . . .

With membership of the United Nations (1955) barely a reality and that of a wider Europe still in the future, for much of the decade Britain remained, for many, the limit of the apprehensible universe. This perception was rich in dichotomies: on the one hand the term 'West Briton' was still the current coin of opprobrium; 'BÁS DON BÉARLA', proclaimed the *Aiséirí* posters. A Radio Éireann announcer, Patrick Begley, was dispensed with after widespread criticism of his 'English' accent. Attempts were made to prevent the showing of the film of Queen Elizabeth II's coronation. And no property developer, had the species existed, would have risked identifying his new suburban estate as some corner of a foreign field with a name such as Cowper Downs,

Chase or Manor. On the other hand, the Kavanaghs – or Patrick, at least – saw in English life, letters and society all that Ireland lacked: 'The last good parties here were thrown by the British during the war. . . . The British have a sense of social living. In London a party is not confined to stupid people as it is here'. Foreign trade meant, virtually, trade with Britain, which supplied not only the bulk of imported goods (if you could afford it you could have any car you liked, provided it was British and black) but also the equipment for what Seán Ó Faoláin termed in 1951 'a joke army, a joke navy and a joke air force'. 'When on this recent Easter Sunday the pinchbeck squadrons of our Bomber Command [sic] roared over our heads', wrote Patrick Kavanagh in 1952, 'the sensitive man could not but feel embarrassed. We did not manufacture those planes. As a military force we would stand no chance and we should not be flaunting our red flag in the face of the bull of the world'.

If the Kavanaghs represented the kind of undifferentiated dissidence which habitually seasons Irish pub-talk, more specific issues were called into question by committed dissident groups. Though the terms of left and right had then very little meaning in the context of Irish politics ('Draw a line', Jack White of the *Irish Times* told a foreign enquirer, 'and put all the parties well to the right. And the Labour Party? Put that furthest of all.'), a controversy under the title 'The Liberal Ethic' in the correspondence columns of the same paper in 1950 revealed a healthy growth of liberal-socialist opinion flourishing in a prevailingly conservative and theocratic climate. The battle of ideas was initially joined between, on the right, Rev Professor Feilim Ó Briain, of University College, Galway, and, on the left, Dr Owen Sheehy Skeffington, lecturer in French at Trinity College, Dublin. 'The future historian of "The Development of Modern Ireland" ', suggested another correspondent, '. . . will undoubtedly attach to the "liberal ethic" correspondence . . . a great significance'. The judgment was not misplaced, since not only did this represent the first real popular statement of the dissident position in the post-war period, but from its particularised origins (the equation by Professor Ó Briain of liberal-socialist views with 'free morality

— the ethics of free love'), it ranged over the main issues of the day — the censorship; the nature of Irish society ('the real trouble in Ireland seems to be "sexophobia" '); the role of Protestants in the Republic ('. . . excluding Catholics from their better-paid posts'); the Westmeath County Council's resolution to amend Article 44 of the Constitution ('Thereby putting the one true church, founded by our Divine Redeemer, on a plane above the man-made religions of the world'); and the nature and purpose of the right-wing organisation Maria Duce, which, at the time of the visit of the comedian Danny Kaye, circulated postcards stating 'Catholic Dublin will keep out this Masonic, Jewish Communist'. (Catholic Dublin's response was well-expressed in a concurrent 'Odearest' advertisement: 'Cried the folk at the plane "Don't be coy/Your stay you are bound to enjoy/For after great thought/ This ODEAREST we've bought/As a present for you, Danny Boy" '.)

Both the thematic and temporal span of the 'Liberal Ethic' correspondence — it ran from 26 January for nearly three months — is to be seen in the context of the absence of any alternative forum for the public debate of major issues. Radio Éireann was dipping a toe gingerly into the maelstrom, initiating a series of unscripted but otherwise formal debates; but in 1951 a contributor to *The Bell* alleged that 'Irish radio . . . has never discussed, say, censorship, The County Management System, Secondary Education. . . .' The issues raised by the so-called Battle of Baltinglass, involving the refusal of the postmistress to accept the dictates of the Department of Posts and Telegraphs, were also denied air-time, as was the Tilson case over the effects on the Protestant minority of the punitive *Ne Temere* decree. The editor of *The Bell* accused that minority of sulking. Rev C.M. Stack responded with the question as to whether he and his co-religionists were really welcome in the Republic, suggesting that many of them supported the maintenance of Partition as offering some guarantees as long as Dublin continued to woo their Northern brethren. But this debate was conducted within the pages of a small-circulation magazine. As far as the country at large was concerned, Catholic-Protestant relationships called for little action other than acceptance of the *status quo*. It was left to a contributor to the Liberal Ethic debate to voice his 'vicarious shame on behalf of one's Roman Catholic friends when seeing them lurking among the tombstones, or peering fearfully through the open door of the church where the Burial Service of a Protestant friend or relative is being conducted'. Such had been the conduct of Mr Costello and his ministers, in effect if not in detail, during the funeral service in 1949 in St Patrick's Cathedral, Dublin, for Ireland's first President, Dr Douglas Hyde.

The character of the decade, however, is something other than the sum of its negations. The groundwork was laid for many developments which were to come to full fruition with the working of the Whitaker miracle, and there were men and women who could forsee for the country a role other than that of provincial backwater and client-state of Britain. Seán MacBride and Erskine Childers, both with origins very different from most of their political contemporaries – as they were from each other – saw Ireland's aspirations against the background of a wider canvas, culturally and politically. Neither had an easy passage. Childers' Radio Éireann Symphony Orchestra was the target of ignorant chauvinism; MacBride's brainchild, the Cultural Relations Committee, was taken to task by the writers of the *Envoy* faction for not doing more to help the struggling artist (the help expected was in most cases pecuniary). MacBride replied that, in his view,

> the Committee is not concerned, except in an indirect fashion, with the welfare of the artist, or even, if I might go so far, with the state of the arts at any given time. . . . Contemporary achievement in the arts is not the beginning and end of our cultural heritage – which did not start with Mr Cronin and his coterie and which will not end with him.

The Tóstal was an attempt within this broader concept of Irish culture to foster international awareness – in this case by bringing visitors to the country – while at the same time creating a new impetus within the community itself. The official attitude was optimistic: 'An Tóstal has been the occasion of initiating a great many new features throughout Ireland', wrote its executive officer in charge of cultural features, Cecil ffrench Salkeld: 'It has also, I am glad to say, been the occasion of reviving and strengthening other features which have existed before in Irish cultural life, but which need just this extra stimulus to become something outstanding'. If the concept did not fulfil official, or indeed popular, expectations (it was in many ways before its time) it can be said to have laid the foundation for the development of the tourist industry which was to follow.

That nascent industry was only slowly freeing itself from the trammels and inhibitions of wartime conditions. 'For travel between Great Britain and Ireland', Fógra Fáilte's new magazine, *Ireland of the Welcomes*, announced in its first issue, May-June 1952, 'no travel papers are required. Since April 7th last, it has been unnecessary for travellers to obtain special documents for travel, or to obtain leave to land from an immigration officer'. In his introduction to the new publication the Taoiseach, Seán Lemass, set the tone that was to permeate the approach to tourism in subsequent decades: 'In Ireland the visitor will find comfortable accommodation, abundance and variety of food, superb sporting facilities, a varied and beautiful landscape — in fact, all the ingredients of a thoroughly enjoyable holiday. Among a friendly, warm-hearted people, he will discover that the famed hospitality is no myth'. *Ireland of the Welcomes* set a high standard from the beginning — contributors to its first half dozen issues included Benedict Kiely, James Laver, Brendan Behan, Lord Dunsany, Donagh McDonagh, Paul Henry, Maurice Walsh — but its advocacy of one aspect of the country's appeal unmentioned by the pragmatic Lemass — the cultural heritage — was not immediately matched by the appropriate local response.

On our first visit to Sligo in the early 1950s, [recalled the English poet, critic and TCD lecturer, Donald Davie] we stayed in the Yeats Country Hotel at Rosses Point, and, when I paid my bill, I gestured towards the portrait of the poet which was the only indication given of what gave the hotel its name. 'Was there', I asked, 'much interest shown in it, or him?' 'Ah no', the young woman assured me, glancing indifferently and rather bemusedly at the picture, to be sure there had been, some years ago. But of late it had all blown over rather.

Davie was to return in later years to direct the highly successful Yeats Summer School, by which time the concept of 'Ireland of the Festivals', pioneered by events such as the Wexford Opera and the International Folk Dance and Song Festival, was well established.

Ireland as a location for film-making, already popularised through productions such as *The Quiet Man*, was again brought into prominence with the shooting, in the summer of 1954, of John Huston's *Moby Dick* in Youghal and his transmogrification of the *Irish Times*'s craggy-faced columnist, Séamus Kelly, into an international, if minor, star. The tourist trade was now being seen, in official circles at least, as something other than simply catering for the British fisherman and his somewhat less élitist compatriots in boarding houses in Bray. *Ireland of the Welcomes* carried a regular page detailing some of the more exotic arrivals, amongst whom was 'Most Rev. Dr. R. O'Donnell, co-adjutor Archbishop of Brisbane [who] recently led a Brisbane Arch-diocesan Pilgrimage to Ireland . . . in Youghal, where the filming of *Moby Dick* is taking place, the Most Rev. Dr. O'Donnell spoke in Irish to a schoolboy'.

That simple scene points to a social environment in which religion and the revival of the language, together with the 'reintegration of the national territory', continued to play a significant, if at times symbolic role. Change was slow, and nowhere more than amongst the classes most seriously affected by economic stagnation and its consequences. The economy was still overwhelmingly agricultural (accounting for 45 per cent of the gainfully employed in 1952), and both on the land and within the very restricted industrial sector, 'the political dimension of working class culture was', in the view of Dónal Nevin, 'almost wholly lacking'. In the period 1945-60, he suggested, there was no discernible class consciousness, rather a status consciousness within classes which was 'probably the main reason for the high degree of trade unionisation, which at 53 per cent of male employees outside agriculture (1952) was one of the highest proportions in the western world'. The Irish worker, in Nevin's view, 'seems to have little sense of public morality'.

Whenever he could get away with it, [said James Plunkett] he limited his output, not because he was lazy or basically dishonest, but because if the same volume of production was done by fewer men, then it was likely that he himself would end up on the breadline. His attitude to trade union negotiation procedures was uncomplicated: serve the demand and, when it was refused (as it usually was) serve strike notice.

This hieratical approach to industrial relations was reflected in the frequency and duration of major industrial disputes during the period. The banks were closed from 23 December 1950 to 16 February 1951 and again in 1954–55; Dublin newspapers did not appear for six weeks in 1952; transport stoppages were endemic. Few of these disruptions caused major inconvenience to a tolerant public which adopted a fatalistic attitude combined with a degree of practical ingenuity reflecting the institutional dimension of the occurrence. In 1953 the Irish National Union of Vintners and the management of Downey's Bar, Dún Laoghaire, agreed settlement terms for a strike which had lasted fourteen years. It was as much a matter of scale as of national temperament: as late as 1958 only forty concerns outside the public service had more than 500 employees. The gradual change that was to manifest itself in labour relations as the decade advanced stemmed from the establishment of the Labour Court in 1946, the first National Wage Agreement of 1948, and the great influx of white collar workers to the trade unions in the mid-fifties.

What industries there were flourished, if that is not too exuberant a term, under the umbrella of protection and were largely modest, family-run concerns content to supply their segment of a small home market in a climate of little or no competition. Clients of one of the few sizable advertising agencies in the early fifties, O'Kennedy-Brindley of Dublin, included a chocolate manufacturer ('Any time is Urney time'), Will's cigarettes, Aspro, Donnelly's sausages and a major Ford dealership, Smithfield Motors, sales-managed by 'Din Joe' Fitzgibbon who, in another incarnation, hosted the popular radio programme *Take the Floor* remarkable for its featuring of Irish dancing, thereby leaving a good deal to the listeners' imagination. Radio was a potent factor not least in advertising: sponsored programmes, pioneered by the Irish Hospitals Sweepstakes' Goodwill Musical Hour, attracted most major consumer advertisers and were to nurture the talents of writers and presenters such as Hugh Leonard, Niall Boden and Gay Byrne. There was, as reflected in the growing prosperity of the agencies (a visualiser moved from O'Kennedy-Brindley to Arks in 1954 at a rumoured salary of £1,000) a recognisable volume of commercial activity, but in many respects it was a rat-race run by mice. 'There is a clearly definable national aspiration to increase the return realised from Ireland's economic activities', concluded the IBEC report in 1952:

> ... paradoxically, along with this actively-voiced ambition for economic betterment, there runs an undercurrent of pessimism or lack of confidence in the prospect for achieving the pronounced aims. The talk is of economic expansion, but the action of the Government, business and labor alike is too often along the lines of consolidating present positions rather than of accepting the hazards inherent in changed practices upon which expansion depends. ... In fact the declarations of expansive purpose are frequently qualified by expressions of a conflicting, anti-materialist philosophy, of an asceticism that opposes material aspirations to spiritual goals, and hence writes down the former as unworthy.

The entrepreneurial spirit was, however, stirring. Hugh McLaughlin's Fleet Publications launched a series of new titles one of which, *Radio Review*, employed novel, and controversial, methods of circulation-building. One of his colleagues, Dónal Ó Moráin, was responsible for the first and most enduring initiative involving a new approach to the revival of Irish since the foundation of the State. His brain-child, Gael Linn,

> in two years has done more for the Irish language than has been done in the previous ten. [said the *Irish Times* in a St Patrick's Day profile in 1956] Only in recent weeks Ó Moráin and Gael Linn have gone into the film-making business. Up to now, virtually no Irish was heard in cinemas ... this will certainly be a boost for the language.

Of the man himself the newspaper said, 'He is what is new in Gaelic circles, a hard-headed and, possibly, hard-hearted businessman'. The same might have been said, with a similar caveat, of another figure of the fifties who walked up the steps of Shanahan's Auction Rooms in Dún Laoghaire one morning in February 1954 with a brilliant idea and the ruthless single-mindedness to pursue it. Paul Singer, a London-domiciled Czechoslovakian-Austrian, persuaded the Shanahan family, who were making a marginal living out of a very depressed property market, to join him in his scheme for becoming one of the world's leading stamp dealers. Within a year 'Green I.S.L.E. Philately' had become, in Dr Singer's own words, 'the sputnik of the philatelic world' and the firm was dealing in millions. The next step was to offer the public at large the opportunity to participate through an ingenious investment system. 'Profit from stamps without risk' proclaimed the publicity, and thousands were induced to part with their savings on the chance of a good return. This, for some considerable time, was exactly what they received. Shanahan's Stamp Auctions appealed not only to the inherent national gambling spirit but shone like a beacon of hope in the drab mid-fifties landscape. Singer had what would now be termed charisma: he operated on a grand scale, both in his business and social life. When the crash came, following a mysterious theft and consequent loss of confidence, causing thousands of investors to clamour for the return of their monies, the Shanahans and Singer were arrested on suspicion of fraud. At the conclusion of lengthy trials in which Paul Singer, conducting his own defence, ran rings round the prosecution, no offence was proven. Dr Singer disappeared as quickly as he had come, leaving behind him not only many who were licking their financial wounds but others who sensed, however tentatively, the stirring of a new spirit of entrepreneurial adventure that was to characterise the sixties.

The markers were being put down. The Industrial Development Authority was established in 1950, the Irish Management Institute, Bord Fáilte and Bord Iascaigh Mhara in 1952, An Foras Talúntais in 1958. In 1952 new social welfare and legal adoption acts were placed on the statute book. The period saw the solid expansion of Irish Shipping, Aer Lingus (the transatlantic service opened in 1958) and Bord na Móna. 'I recall that between 1949 and 1957 in this country we built or reconstructed over 100,000 houses' wrote James Dillon in the Fine Gael *National Observer* in 1959, 'we provided 8,000 additional hospital beds, we provided sufficient sanitoria to provide for all cases of tuberculosis requiring sanatorium treatment, we increased the number of cattle on the land from 3,950,000 to 4,466,000. . . .' In the cultural sphere, 1953 witnessed the opening both of Michael Scott's Busáras, the first building of any significance in Dublin for a century, and the Chester Beatty Library, whilst the establishment of Liam Miller's Dolmen Press in 1951 paved the way for a resurgence of book publishing. Probably no development, however, had more profound a significance than that of rural electrification, ushering in as it did a new way of life which was not, at first, greeted with unqualified enthusiasm. The old methods still retained their devotees: 'What is good enough for Liberace is good enough for me', insisted a rural *bean a'tí* in a contemporary cartoon; another unimpressed customer complained, of the connection charge, 'You could buy a quare lot of candles for seventeen pound'.

'All great civilisations are based on parochialism', said Patrick Kavanagh, drawing his distinction between the provincial (bad) and the parochial (good). By this criterion Ireland in 1948-58 must have held an honoured place, to judge only by the strength of the provincial press and what Hubert Butler described as 'the primitive power of focussing our minds like burning glasses on tiny patches'. Modernisation proceeded piecemeal and by stealth. Motor car registration marks, established under the British régime at the dawn of the automobile era, were still barely into three-letter combinations, and that only in major urban centres. In 1958 the telephone number of the Imperial Hotel, Castlebar, was still Castlebar 3, and one of the attractions of its twenty-five bedrooms and five bathrooms was, an advertisement assured the public, 'electric light'. It was still possible to travel by train from Thurles to Clonmel via Horse and Jockey, from Roscrea to Birr, from Kilfree Junction to James Dillon's Ballaghadereen and, by the unique West Clare, from Ennis to Craggaghknock, Shragh, Moyasta Junction and Kilkee; but in 1948 the fastest train between Dublin and Cork averaged only 37 mph. On the other hand one might drive through Dublin without encountering any delaying impediment other than the flocks of bicycles which constituted a significant segment of commuter transport. In this sector, however, the modes were on the brink of change. The railway system was in what appeared to be terminal decline, with the average age of a CIE carriage forty-seven years and a loco-motive fifty-one. Most of the barely-used branch lines survived until the end of the decade, but Dublin's tramway system did not see the fifties. When the last tram ran from Westmoreland Street to Blackrock depot in the early hours of Monday, 11 July 1949, 'Nothing came in but the ironwork', according to the *Irish Times* report. It was both an affectionate farewell to an efficient, economic and ecologically impeccable system uprooted in the name of progress, and a dim foreshadowing of the new breed of vandalising gurrier about to take the stage: 'Six trams were damaged and three almost totally wrecked; several persons missed electrocution by the merest chance as they clambered on tram rooftops; and some of the residents of Ballsbridge lit a bonfire on the main road'.

When CIE, with its intermittently risible flying-snail symbol, became a fully-fledged State-sponsored body in 1950 all its ser-vices were steam-hauled. Its experimental turf-burning locomotive was to be one of the last completely new steam designs in the world. But the writing was on the wall. The Great Northern Rail-way, after 1953 jointly owned by the Belfast and Dublin govern-ments, had introduced diesel power and in 1951 the first railcars began running between Dublin and Waterford. If the eclipse of steam was sudden and complete the trams, or their evidences, lingered in the shape of half-buried tracks in Dublin streets, a trap for the ubiquitous bicycles. When at last College Green was resurfaced, necessitating its complete closure for a period, it was as if the city had returned to its eighteenth-century apogee. One walked through the front gate of Trinity College as if into a Malton print: no wheeled traffic, nothing but unaccommodating clay extending to the steps of Parliament House.

In other respects the Augustan capital of a Gaelic nation remained largely intact, if notoriously neglected. In September 1951 Maurice Craig suggested that something should be done about the Royal Hospital, Kilmainham, then housing the detritus of the National Museum together with politically unacceptable statues. 'The whole site', he wrote, 'could become a place of resort comparable to Hampton or Kew. . . .' Another scheme designed to add lustre to the life of the city was also under discussion. 'The project of building a concert hall in Dublin', said *The Bell* in January 1952, 'is now one of the oldest war-horses of Irish musical life'. (A scheme based on the Rotunda in Parnell Square had been a casualty of Coalition revisionism in 1948.) Even the supporters of the project were, however, uncertain as to whether a demand existed ('We, the musical Irish, are musical only potentially . . .'); but there was no such uncertainty regarding the cinemas, queues for which shuffled their way into the Royal, the Carlton, the Adelphi, the Savoy, good film or bad, hail, rain or shine. Though suffering the castigations of the critics ('We are in one of the worst slumps imaginable as far as theatrical talent is concerned', complained *Envoy*), the Abbey, Gate and Olympia (and after September 1953 the brave and innovative Pike) continued to hold their audiences, with the shilling seats at the Gate particularly attractive to the impecunious student, who might even slip a copper into the collecting box shaken under his nose by the substantial figure of the Earl of Longford.

Longford — impresario, poet, translator and landed gentleman — was one of a group who were in more ways than one larger than life. None larger, of course, than Brendan Behan:

> There are persons of bourgeois respectability in the city of Dublin [wrote the *Irish Times* in October 1956] who nourish a secret unease. It is that one day they may be proceeding on their middle-class way, chatting smoothly with their employer or their bank manager, when suddenly from across the street will come a loud and ebullient 'View-Halloo', followed by a colourful and uninhibited commentary on things in general. . . .

Another earl — Wicklow — publisher and pioneer of stately home hospitality (his paying guests stole the silver) was numbered amongst a company of which the chief luminary, not least in his own estimation, was the Pope O'Mahony – commoner, one felt, only under constraint. Few have so successfully combined paunch and panache. 'The span-long reference book entries . . . read not so much like a bleak, Who's whosy biography of a private individual as the account, rendered down, of a Celtic clan, a European dynasty and a twelve-decker club sandwich'. The Pope's ability to appear in the most unlikely places at equally unlikely times made one suspect, at the very least, bilocation; but in his capacity, or capacities, as a walking Almanach de Gotha, the circle of whose acquaintance appeared to take in half the nearly-crowned heads of Europe (he was an advocate of the restoration of a native Irish monarchy) he was socially irresistible, if, even by the standards of the backward-looking fifties, something of a splendid anachronism.

As was, in many respects, the decade itself. The rest of the world had moved on, and there were many in Ireland who were leaving to join it. For those who stayed, there was the apparently perennial presence of Éamon de Valera, 'The man', the London *Observer* wrote in 1957,

> who not only embodies the continuity with the early turbulent years but also makes sense of them. When Irishmen begin to doubt whether the Rising, the 1919 election, the Black and Tan period, the Civil War and all the rest of it makes any sense at all against the background of present-day Ireland with its partition and continuing emigration, there is 'Dev' with his presence, his pedantic manner and devious phrases taking for granted that it does and showing them expertly how the sum is done.

There were others, however, who were doing their own sums, working to rid the nation of the Joycean paralysis, creating, however tentatively, the climate that was to establish the conditions for the Whitaker initiative and all that flowered therefrom. It was not, when all is said and done, the worst of times. In 1957 Conor Cruise O'Brien did some research amongst Northern unionist schoolchildren on their attitude to Ireland. 'The people are pretty well civilised', concluded one of their number, 'and

there are not often many brutle mudders'.
    Perhaps we should leave it at that.

John A. Costello (courtesy G.A. Duncan)

Seán MacBride (courtesy G.A. Duncan)

Index

Sheehy-Skeffington, Dr Owen 159
Sheffield University 152
Singer, Dr Paul 166
Single European Market 142
Sinn Féin 37, 78, 129
Smith, Patrick 55
Smith, Terence 155
Stack, Rev C.M. 160
Stalin, Joseph 115, 122
Statist, the 108
Statistical and Social Inquiry Society
   of Ireland 14, 41, 44, 70, 95,
   100, 149
   Journal of, 149, 150
Stuart, Francis 155
Studies 108, 123, 156
Sunday Press, the 158
Sweetman, Gerard 14, 24-5, 33-4,
   36, 42-3, 67, 68-9, 88-91, 93,
   121-22
Synge, J.M. 81

Take the Floor 164
TCD 152
Thatcher, Margaret 150
*Third Programme for Economic Ex-
   pansion* 133-4
Tierney, Michael 82
Tilson case, the 160
Tóstal, an 152, 155, 161-2
Treaty, the 17, 78, 80, 83, 150
Trinity College, Dublin 54, 83, 87,
   112, 123, 152, 159, 162, 168
Truman, President 116

United Nations 34, 89, 92, 158
United States Department of State
   19
University College, Dublin 68, 83,
   87, 112

University College, Galway 159
University Philosophical Society 153

Vaizey, John 33
Vanishing Irish, the 25, 156
Vanoni Plan 26, 39, 89, 122

Walsh, Brendan 75, 77, 106, 109
Walsh, Maurice 162
Way Forward, the 136
Wexford Opera Festival 163
Whitaker, T.K. 11-12, 14-17, 20, 22-
   3, 26, 29, 32, 38-63, 67, 69, 70,
   71, 75, 82, 84, 85, 89-91, 95-
   105, 108, 109, 114, 121-24, 125,
   130, 132, 143, 149, 150, 161, 170
   Whitaker Plan 11, 28, 38-63, 74
   Whitaker Memorandum 48-53,
   108
White, Jack 159
White Paper, 1965, see *First Pro-
   gramme for Economic Expansion*
Wicklow, Earl of 169
Williams, Desmond 108
Woodrow Wilson School of Public
   and International Affairs 67
Woods, Thomas, see Thomas Hogan
Working with Europe 19
World Bank 49, 90, 92, 95, 98, 101
   Economic Development Institute
   of, 92
World War II 78, 80, 82, 83, 84,
   114-115, 149, 152, 154

Yeats, W.B. 154, 162
   Yeats Summer School 163
Yom Kippur War 140